Parenting from the Heart

Selected Articles from
Motherwear's Magazine
for Nurturing Families

Parenting from the Heart

Selected Articles from
Motherwear's Magazine
for Nurturing Families

♥

Published by Motherwear, Inc.,
Northampton, Massachusetts

Parenting from the Heart
Selected Articles from Motherwear's Magazine
for Nurturing Families
Compiled by Ziporah Hildebrandt
Edited by Carolyn Dash Mailler
Designed by Lynn Zimmerman

Copyright 1996 by Motherwear, Inc.,
320 Riverside Drive, Northampton, MA, 01060
(413) 586-1978

ISBN: 0-9649867-0-1 14.95
Library of Congress Cataloging in Publication Data:
Parenting from the Heart: Selected Articles from
Motherwear's Magazine for Nurturing Families
Mailler, Carolyn Dash, ed.
236pp. 25.4cm. $14.95

1. Parenting 2. Attachment Parenting 3. Parenting Young Children
I. Title
Library of Congress Catalog Card Number: 95-81645

*Front cover photos (from top) courtesy of Amy Cassotta,
the Smith-Boves, Carrie G. Costello & Pekka Hall,
Margaret Kelsey Wright, and Denise Morris.
Back cover photo courtesy of Jody Wright.*

To Olisa, Mahajoy, Sundarii, Liina, and Emily
for teaching me everything I know about parenting,
and to Prakash for sharing it all with me. — JW

To my husband, Carl,
and our children, Kiersten and Carson,
who fill every day of my life with love. — CDM

Contents

CHAPTER ONE
Loving, Caring, and Bonding

Showing Love to Our Children, by Jody Wright 3

Marsupial Parenting, by Beth Hersh 5

Listening to Babies, by Vimala McClure 7

Forming a Loving Bond with Your Baby, by Jody Wright 11

Seeing Them Whole, by Beth Hersh 14

Why Your Baby Loves to Be Touched, by Jody Wright 17

Take a Bath with Your Baby, by Ziporah Hildebrandt 20

Want to Massage Your Baby? Just Do It! by Jody Wright 22

Infant Massage: A Way to Show You Care, by Jody Wright 23

Babies Love Sounds, by Ziporah Hildebrandt 25

"And Then What Happened?" Telling Stories to Children,
    by Ziporah Hildebrandt 27

The Most Perfect Baby in the Whole Wide World, by Jody Wright 30

CHAPTER TWO
Breastfeeding

The Magic of Milk, by Beth Hersh 35

Why Is Breastfeeding So Important? by Jody Wright 37

The Message Is Love, by Beth Hersh 39

The Elements of Breastfeeding Success, by Jody Wright 40

Mothers Share: Our readers discuss The Challenges of Nursing,
    compiled by Jody Wright 43

Lay a Strong Foundation for Breastfeeding Success,
    by Ziporah Hildebrandt 48

The Amazing Health Benefits of Nursing, by Jody Wright 50

Nursing the Adopted Baby, by Jody Wright 52

Tandem Nursing, by Amy Mager 54

Mothers Share: Our readers discuss Expressing Milk,
    compiled by Jody Wright 57

How Breastfeeding Saves You Money, by Jody Wright 61

The Art of Discreet Nursing, by Jody Wright 64

Mothers Share: Our readers discuss Nursing in Public,
    compiled by Jody Wright 66

When It's Time to Wean, by Beth Hersh 69

CHAPTER THREE
Parenting

Something Wonderful About Toddlers, by Beth Hersh 75

Helping Children Express Their Feelings, by Jody Wright......................... 77

Becoming a Sibling, by Beth Hersh 79

Treating Children as Equals, by Jody Wright 82

A Fine Line: Popular Culture and Our Children,
    by Ziporah Hildebrandt 85

Magic Moments, by Beth Hersh... 89

The Tao of Motherhood, excerpted from the book
    by Vimala McClure 91

CHAPTER FOUR
Survival

Getting Ready for the First Six Weeks,
    compiled by Jody Wright.. 96

The Challenges of Parenting a Baby, by Jody Wright 100

Colic and Allergy: a Trying Time, by Ziporah Hildebrandt 101

Dealing with Postpartum Blues, by Judy Snyder 104

Surviving Postpartum Depression 106

How to Survive a Fussy Baby, by Beth Hersh 109

Don't Sweat It: Tips for Summer Sanity, by Andrea Collins 113

Taking It Out on the Kids, by Beth Hersh 115

Mothers Share: Our readers discuss Handling Criticism,
    compiled by Jody Wright 118

A Nursing Mom's Holiday Survival Guide, by Ziporah Hildebrandt 120

Our Little Lamb Is a Goat, by Carol Hubbard House 123

CHAPTER FIVE
Sleep

How Does Your Baby Sleep? by Jody Wright 131

Uncovering the Myths About Shared Beds, by Beth Hersh 133

Does She Sleep Through the Night? by Judi Hammett 135

Mothers Share: Our readers discuss Sleep Patterns,
    compiled by Jody Wright 138

Baby's Sleep Needs and You, by Ziporah Hildebrandt 143

Lullabies, by Denise A. Berg 146

CHAPTER SIX
Health and Safety

Wholesome Ways to Feed Your Little One, by Beth Hersh 150

Some Thoughts on Cutting the Food Budget, by Beth Hersh 153

Learning About Homeopathy, by Michele Sellner Paine 156

The Healing Team, by Beth Hersh 158

Protecting Kids from the Sun, by Ziporah Hildebrandt 160

Dressing Your Baby for Cold Weather,
    by Ziporah Hildebrandt 162

CHAPTER SEVEN
Diapering

A Whirlwind Tour of Diapering, by Ziporah Hildebrandt 166

Cotton Diapers: Better for Baby, Better for the World,
    by Dayna Hamp 169

Mothers Share: Our readers discuss Diaper Laundering,
    compiled by Jody Wright 173

Diapers: Comfort, Convenience, and Health, by Ziporah Hildebrandt 176

What to Do About Diaper Rash, by Ziporah Hildebrandt 178

CHAPTER EIGHT
Lifestyles

Home Birth, by Sheryl Stettes Kramer 182

Choreographing a Family, by Jody Wright 184

Practical Tips for the First Two Years,
    compiled by Ziporah Hildebrandt 187

My Four Miracles, by Jody Wright 190

Why Pets Matter, by Beth Hersh 194

The Visitor, by Allena James 196

Mothers Share: Our readers discuss Fathers at Home,
    compiled by Jody Wright 198

Is Working at Home for You? by Jody Wright 201

Mothers Share: Our readers discuss Saving Money,
    compiled by Jody Wright 205

Baby Camping, by Diane Greening 208

The Best Toy Ever, by Ziporah Hildebrandt 210

Carriers, by Dayna J. Hamp 213

The Home Learning Alternative, by Jody Wright 214

TV: We're Working It Out, by Ziporah Hildebrandt 217

CHAPTER NINE
You

The Baby and the Appointment Book, by Theresa Rodriguez Farrisi 222

Take a Break, by Jody Wright 226

Exercising During Pregnancy—and After, by Alicia McDonald 229

Time Management for Moms, by Jody Wright 231

Foreword

Parenting is a personal journey to a unique destination. It is filled with inspiration, rewards, and endless wonder—and its share of trials and errors as well. Advice, from the sound to the absurd, is everywhere we turn, but adopting other people's methods is useless if, in the end, we haven't followed our hearts. Trusting love and intuition to guide us through our child-raising years is the very definition of parenting from the heart.

Sometimes a reminder to trust your intuition is all you need to carry on. This book provides that inspiration with the combined wisdom of those immersed in parenting. Here you will find articles to educate, inspire, support, and even surprise you, as a family of mothers shares determination, fear, joy, tears, and success. You won't doubt for a minute that they are parenting from their hearts; love for their children comes shining through on every page.

photo courtesy of Kathy A. Hemberger

Loving, Caring, and Bonding

At the heart of any deep relationship is a phenomenon called bonding. It occurs when science meets mysticism, when biology embraces wonder. Infants need bonding for survival, and connecting with their babies is what nature intended parents to do.

Successful bonding makes good families. It employs emotional and physical responses and an ability to communicate. It is loving and trusting and understanding one another, and it is more. Bonding speaks through the mysterious peace that settles over a mother as her baby nurses at her breast. It gives two hearts the knowledge to handle each new phase of life together.

Bonding makes it easy to love and care for our babies. It makes us want to give, no matter how little sleep we've gotten, no matter how much pain we may be in. It is only part magic; the rest is in our hands.

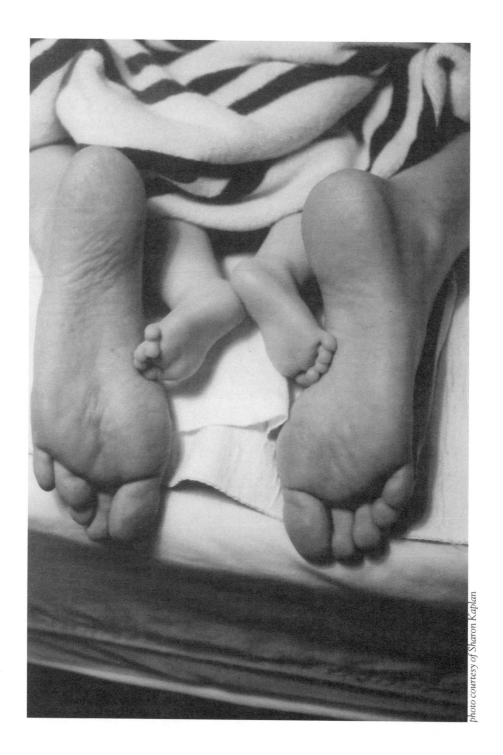

Showing Love to Our Children

BY JODY WRIGHT

Last night I lay next to my nine-year-old and held her hand as, in the darkness, the many questions she had been pondering emerged: "Mom, what happens after we die?" "Why do they put chlorine in pools?" "My hair used to be shorter than Mahajoy's, how come it's longer now?"

My seven-year-old is a little more elusive. I have to catch her early in the morning or late in the evening, when she is open to a snuggle, and tell her how special she is to me, how I am so happy that she is my daughter. That's when she opens up.

My youngest is easy; in fact, with her there is no choice. When she needs a hug she searches me out and crawls into my lap. I am hers and she is mine; there is no doubt about it.

I find that if I make sure to fill the love needs of each of my children every morning, the whole day goes more smoothly. Then, if one of them misbehaves during the day, special time with Mom or Dad usually resolves it.

There are three very specific things that you can do to show your children you love them. First, give them your complete attention. We aren't trained to do this very well in our culture. We see children as getting in the way, keeping us from doing important things. We don't slow down to their pace and open our hearts to their needs.

I've found that when I take family time or time alone with a child, we often start out by expressing anger or feeling ill at ease. If we patiently plow through these accumulated frustrations, we soon become more open, peaceful, and loving.

Second, make eye contact. When we look right into people's eyes, we let them know that we respect them, that they are important to us, that we are being honest with them and they can trust us. It is easy to talk down to children. To show your love, sit down at their level or bring them up to yours. Even dressing a child while making eye contact and talking about the day conveys your love.

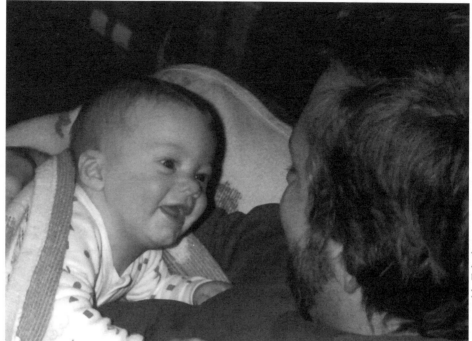

photo courtesy of the Tubachs

The third way to show love, and perhaps the most powerful, is through touch. When I train teachers of infant massage, we do an exercise in which we share a memory of touch that was important to us. Most people remember something from their childhood. " I loved it when my grandmother used to comb my hair," or "My father was so surprised to see me that he gave me this great big hug. I had never felt so loved by him before." But often what comes up is sadness at the lack of touch, a memory of a great longing to be held and touched that wasn't satisfied. I think we are designed to be touched. It is a fundamental part of our humanness. Touch is soothing and reassuring. It lets us know we are safe. Most of all, it lets us know we are loved.

For a baby, touch means being held, carried, nursed, and physically comforted in response to her cry. As a child gets older, touch is a hug to start the day, an embrace after a fall, a massage at bedtime. A teenager needs a warm pat on the back for a job well done, or a hug before and after a long absence.

We know we love our children, but they don't always feel loved. They need—and deserve—to be reminded. Our children want to be told they are loved, but most of all they want to be shown. ♥

Marsupial Parenting

BY BETH HERSH

Before babies are born they are encompassed in the safe and contained world of the womb. While we attend to our tasks, we think now and then to pat them and speak love through the skin and tissue that seem to separate us. They have all they need: warmth, food, motion, security, and sensory stimulation. They hear the steady rhythm of our heartbeats and the muffled sounds of our lives. They see bits of light and feel the strong, pulsing umbilical cord, all within the context of Mommy.

Then they are born into the real world, where parents have chores, commitments, and responsibilities. The first few days we sit with them, rock them, nurse them; before long, the real world begins to get in the way.

So what do we do with our babies? Manufacturers offer a vast array of items to contain and amuse them. With cribs, playpens, infant seats, swings, bouncing seats, and walkers, they promise that babies can be safely accommodated, leaving parents free to do what needs to be done.

And these work: The baby is happy some of the time. Other times she fusses and cries and clings and won't settle no matter where you put her or what you hang in front of her. This usually happens when dinner needs to be made, the other children crave your attention, or the phone rings with that call you've been waiting for.

There is a better way — a way that has been around as long as there have been babies. It is designed to continue the attachment of a newborn and her mother. I call it "marsupial parenting," because it works like a kangaroo's pouch. When a baby kangaroo is born he is too underdeveloped and vulnerable to survive without a lot of protection. He crawls up the mother's belly and slips into her pouch. There he finds her nipples and feeds and snuggles until he grows enough to be safe in the world.

photo courtesy of Denise Evarts

When you carry your baby close to your body, she experiences this same kind of comfort. By being close, she can share your warmth, smell your familiar smell, and hear your heartbeat. As you go through your day, she can relax into your movement and be both comforted and stimulated by the sound of your voice. When she grows a little stronger, you can shift your "pouch" to your back where she will see new and exciting things. Then, your hands and arms will be free for more involved tasks.

It might seem like a tremendous amount of work to carry your baby wherever you go, and at times it is overwhelming. But the more she is involved with the family, the sooner the others can form relationships with her and she with them. From this will come a sense of confidence and willingness for adventure, and she will soon be ready to take her place beside you in your active world. ♥

Listening to Babies

BY VIMALA McCLURE

My work with parents and their infants over the last twelve years has confirmed to me that babies have three common needs: they need to agree with their caregivers, they need sensory signals from their caregivers, and they need to be heard. When these three needs (which overlap) are met, the baby radiates health, well-being, and contentment, regardless of his or her temperament.

Joseph Chilton Pearce, in *Magical Child Matures*, emphasizes that children are innately driven to "follow the model" their parents present for them. He explains that an infant's inner blueprint for development holds all the possibilities for its reality. However, the particular experiences that child has depends on what is reflected back by his models. The inner blueprint pushes the infant to search for those mirrors and interact with them.

For example, if an infant of a Spanish-speaking mother is placed with a Swahili-speaking mother, the structure of his language will be Swahili. The possibility for *any* language is within the child's universal internal blueprint; the mirror placed in front of him, in the form of the caregiver model, brings out the particular configuration of that child's expression of his or her inner blueprint. The models that are not presented cause that part of the blueprint to atrophy; it is much more difficult to learn another language after the stage-specific period.

When we apply this idea on the emotional and spiritual levels, we can begin to see the importance of subtle cues we give our infants. This is not a mechanistic process; rather, it is holistic—it takes in the whole being rather than just a part, such as the intellect. Therefore, a parent who presents a model of intellectual achievement to the child can unfold that child's blueprint for high intelligence, but without a corresponding sensitivity to the child's other needs, what develops is a highly intelligent person who is emotionally and spiritually crippled.

When we affirm a baby's wholeness right from the start, the baby grows in confidence and trust. How is this done? By conveying respect, focused attention, honesty, and unconditional love in our interactions with infants.

The parent who doesn't believe her baby has a capacity for interaction or that is not "smart" enough to process environmental cues and stimuli is careless in her baby's presence. The infant gets the message: I am not worthy of respect. Conflict arises between the infant's inborn blueprint, which assumes limitlessness as a given, and the messages he gets from the parent, with whom he is driven to agree.

Out of this conflict can arise frustration and then anger, or depression and hopelessness. Because of the way our society is structured, we rarely notice her frustration until the child has grown to adulthood, when her state of being counts for more because of her capacity to contribute to society as a whole. Then we notice in a big way people who are unable to give or who persist in self-defeating behaviors which wreak havoc on everyone around them.

Infants are designed by nature for a specific sequence of events that unlocks the blueprint of limitlessness they carry within. At birth, they are alert and ready to go; the stress hormones produced at the beginning of labor have helped create massive numbers of new connecting links between the neurons in a baby's brain.

The baby is primed for all the new learning that will happen in the coming months. However, if the stress hormones continue to be produced in the baby's body, this prime-time is lost; a kind of shock ensues wherein the brain shuts down. The baby withdraws into sleep and will be irritable and non-interactive for the first four to six weeks of life.

The infant's brain needs certain signals to tell it to stop producing stress hormones immediately after birth. These signals come from the mother's sensory system and include eye contact, the scent of her body, and the sound of her voice. When the infant receives these signals, the stress hormones stop, and the baby is ready to use all those new connections in the brain. This baby will be responsive and interactive within forty-eight hours of birth. His delightful signals back to mother and her responses begin the dance of bonding. Mother continues to provide sensory cues, varying and adapting them to each stage of the baby's development. She thus allows the baby's inner blueprint to unfold within the relative safety of stimuli which are known to him, and from which he can venture out slowly to take in the rest of the world.

Babies who have been stressed by—or after—birth, for whatever reason, are not, however, doomed to less-than-optimal emotional and spiritual development. A conscious parent can be patient with the infant who has withdrawn, providing a safe, understanding space within which the baby can slowly open up.

Too often, because the parent also suffers from stress (and a less-than-optimal

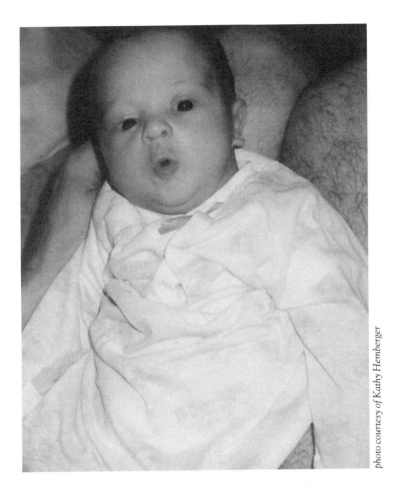

photo courtesy of Kathy Hemberger

infancy of her own), the parent becomes frustrated with her infant's lack of response and comes to the conclusion that the baby doesn't like her or that the baby is incapable of understanding. She begins to feel helpless and inadequate and, without really intending to, models frustration to the baby.

Mothers whose babies are in day care often become alienated from their infants because the infant is so much "better" with the baby-sitter. Recently, a mother of a premature baby in day care said to me, "I don't know what I'm doing wrong. He just seems to like the baby-sitter more than he likes me. He is so happy and calm with her, and at home he cries all the time." She had begun to feel negativity toward her baby and to allow him to cry for long periods alone in his crib. I shared with her an observation that babies in day care often save up their negativity, fears, and anger for their mothers, with whom they feel safe. It was a demonstration of *trust* on his part, not alienation. This simple understanding changed their whole relationship. She was able to go to him with love again, and listen to his troubles. Her personal power as Mother was restored, and this enabled her to give beyond what she had been perceiving as her limit. The baby's crying began to diminish as he started to feel heard.

Advances in psychological research are beginning to show us that infants are far more capable of understanding what goes on around them than we ever thought they were. Babies process information in a different manner, just as children differ from adults in the way they interpret experiences. I am convinced that infants absorb the underlying energies or messages of events and people around them, most specifically that all-important source of information, the parent. In addition, babies have feelings of their own and a need to express them.

When I begin to talk about infant conversations in my infant massage seminars, I like to start with an analogy, usually acted out by participants. Imagine you have just been through a very traumatic experience, something that really disturbed you deeply. You feel yourself on the verge of tears and unable to relax or concentrate, and you go to your spouse or a friend for help. You begin to talk about what happened to you and how you're feeling about it.

After a moment of sympathy your friend begins to shush you, saying, "There, there, never mind. Please don't cry. I can't stand it when you cry. Come on, smile for me now. Let me get you something to eat. Maybe you should go to a doctor." You will probably dry your tears and internalize your pain in order to preserve this relationship. Your friend's responses have told you it is not safe to be yourself in her presence.

Now imagine yourself in the same situation, with a different response from your friend. You begin to talk about what happened to you and how you're feeling about it. Your friend looks at you eye-to-eye. She leans forward and holds your hand. "I'm here for you," she says. "Tell me all about it. I can see you're really hurting, and I want you to know that I love you and I want to help you through this."

She puts her arms around you and you relax into deep sobs in the safety of her presence. You ramble on, sometimes incoherently, and she's there, saying, "Tell me more. And then what happened? That must have been so painful for you." You feel her genuine support, and that trust enables you to really unload and, finally, come back to your center again. Your relationship with her is stronger; she feels good for having been there for you, and you are better able to go on toward healthy functioning.

I have seen many remarkable instances in which an infant's responsiveness and general disposition have completely changed after being truly heard. Infants need to be heard as much as anyone. ♥

Forming a Loving Bond
with Your Baby

BY JODY WRIGHT

Our first child's birth mother called us when she was still in labor, and it wasn't long before we were holding our daughter-to-be. I remember some precious moments of that day when I sat with Olisa asleep on my lap. I looked at her little face and memorized her widely spaced eyes, her thick, shiny black hair, her almondy brown skin. I took her into my heart and vowed to always care for and protect her. Our relationship grew from there.

What is bonding? What is this process of attachment and empathy for another being that ties you together no matter what? Bonding, whether with a partner, a baby you birth, or an adopted child or stepchild is really about forming family, about developing the intimacy and trust that make families so special.

I have explored bonding by looking at the different parent-baby interactions that Dr. Marshall Klaus and Dr. John Kennell defined in their trail-breaking research on bonding. Possibly the most important of these interactions is touch. Babies and mothers are in constant contact before birth. While the birthing process separates a baby from the womb, it needn't separate her from her mother's familiar touch. Often the new form of contact begins with a mother touching her infant's extremities with her fingertips. Then she moves toward the trunk of her baby's body. How similar this is to the process of developing a romantic relationship: touching tentatively, holding hands, and then gaining confidence and intimacy.

Babies and their parents also connect by making eye contact immediately after birth. What an amazing thing it is to see a newborn so alert and aware! Dimmed lights, time alone, and a safe and familiar environment help pave the way for these special moments that start a loving connection.

Voice is another important mode of bonding. A baby hears the voices of his mother and others around him throughout the last months of pregnancy. After

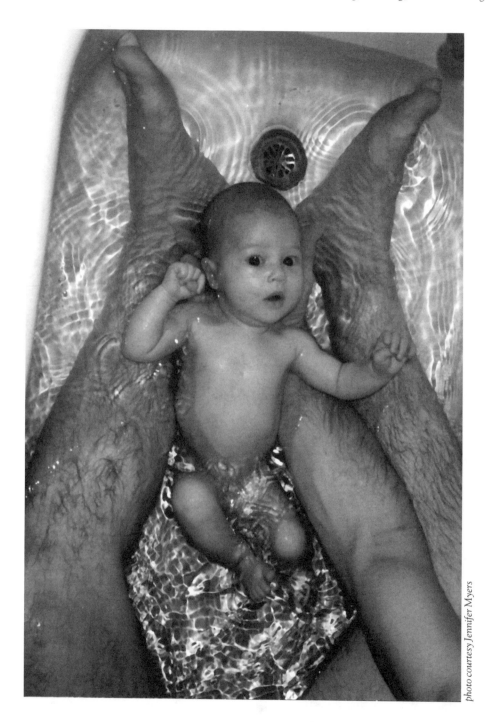

birth, he begins to associate faces with these voices. And even newborns seem to move in synchronicity to the speech of those around them, raising an eyebrow or moving a foot in response to a syllable.

Babies are born already familiar with the rhythm of their mothers' lives. This harmony is one of the natural bonds between them. Unfortunately, hospital routines can disrupt this bond, particularly if mother and child are separated.

Breastfeeding provides several ways to strengthen the bond of mother and child. The baby's sucking releases hormones in the mother, which help her body return to normal and aid her ability to parent her child. These hormones relax the mother and give her pleasure, which encourages her to nurse longer and to love being with her child. In turn, nursing releases hormones that relax a baby as he nurses, often putting him to sleep. The mother provides antibodies, digestive aids, and natural laxatives through her milk to help her baby become strong and healthy. In addition, the bacteria on her body help the baby adjust gradually to the swarm of organisms that he will soon encounter elsewhere.

Smell is an important part of the bonding process. Within a few days of birth, babies recognize the smell of their mothers. Mothers love to smell the wonderful musk that emanates from their own babies' bodies, particularly their heads. Perhaps cradle cap is actually an excessive secretion of this natural musk oil.

Finally, heat plays a part in bonding: the warmth of his mother's body is the perfect temperature for a newborn, and much more reliable than an unresponsive hospital warming light. The best thing to do with a healthy newborn is place him on his mother's chest with a warmed blanket on top. Pure bliss!

Obviously, the most conducive environment for bonding is one in which parents and baby are allowed plenty of time alone together in a warm, relaxed place, with complete freedom to breastfeed. But what can you do if those ideal circumstances don't exist? You can work to recreate these same interactions with a child, whether it is two weeks, two months, or two years later: privacy, touch, eye contact, communication through voice, common biorhythms, nursing or closeness during feeding, sharing of smells, and warmth. Infant massage, sharing a bed, adoptive nursing, taking a bath together, and quiet moments in a rocking chair are ideal ways to build a relationship. The beautiful intimacy that results is the foundation of a loving family. ♥

Seeing Them Whole

BY BETH HERSH

The other day, a friend and I were talking about our kindergarten-age daughters, who each have very visible differences from most children. We were talking about their emotional development, and what it will be like for them when they reach the age when children stop being curious about others who are different and start fearing them, instead. This is the age when self-consciousness begins and they suddenly find their security in looking like everyone else. Our children do not look like everyone else. In a very few years, that's going to matter to them and their peers.

I work in an institution with children who need assistance to eat, to move; some, even to breathe. These children are isolated from the community because of the special care they need and, more likely, because they are hard to look at, hard to get close to, painful to accept. I care for them; I change them, dress them, position them in bed or in wheelchairs. I've been doing it for over a year, and still I sometimes have a hard time just being close to them. I read their charts, I know their tragic stories. I know their ages and I compare what a whole child of their age would be doing. I go home sometimes and cry for them.

A friend once told me that the reason I was having such a hard time with these children was that I was feeling sorry for them instead of loving them. What seemed to me to be compassion was really getting in their way and in my way of helping them grow. He said that children know when you see them as not okay and it doesn't matter that you may love them. If you see them as not whole, they sense it on some level and they feel anger and pain about it.

I didn't understand that at all. How could compassion get in the way of helping them? Isn't pity, isn't sorrow what motivates me to care for them so gently and so thoroughly?

"No," he said. He explained that looking at them with sorrow, or worse, with pity, implies that they are not okay, that they are somehow diminished, that they are less than whole. Seeing them as less than whole makes them almost less than

photo courtesy of the Longmores

human. How can I really love them if I don't even recognize that which is our bond, that which is identical between their beings and my own?

He said, "When you look at a cloud floating in the sky you don't say, 'Oh, what a poor thing, being only a cloud.' You don't look at a horse grazing in a field and say, 'Poor horse. If only you could be whole.' Because they *are* whole."

That's the point in the conversation where I lost it. "But, but, but...." I stuttered. "But the cloud is a perfect example of a cloud and the horse is a whole being of a horse!"

"And these are whole children," he said to me.

My task became to go back and learn to see them as no different than me. To search in their bodies and faces to find what is essential to them, to me, to us as humans. I started with the obvious. They have beating hearts, flowing blood, nerves, feelings. They smile when they're happy, they laugh when amused. They cry, they release emotionally when a situation becomes too much for them. Still, what I searched for was harder to define using my mind. I really needed to use my heart to feel the essence of who they really are, and to see how they are no different than me.

It was an intuitive leap and it took a while to really feel it. But when I was able to understand it, it made all the difference. It suddenly became more important to talk to them, to "converse" with them during their care. It became essential to try to reach each one of them on some level every time I touched them, even if telepathic empathy was all the link they were capable of.

Learning this at work, I tried to bring it home to my little one and her friend. How often when I looked at my child did I see her differences and not her glowing child-ness? How much did the sight of her "distortions" keep me from recognizing her true beauty? The truth is that she is a whole being. Whole and complete and beautiful. Exactly as she is. It is my choice what I see when I look at her. If I look at her face, that doesn't move the same as another child's, my reaction to her is sadness. What does that do to her self-esteem, to so often have sadness projected at her, no matter how often I cover it with a smile and tell her I love her? She knows when I am simply loving her, and when my love is tinged with grief. She doesn't express it openly, perhaps she isn't even consciously aware of it, but I believe she knows. It's important for me to be aware of what I choose every time I look at her.

This is not denial. Her father and I recognize that we have a difficult situation to deal with and we make sure we get the proper medical care and therapy for her. We discuss it with her and with her sisters when they mention it and communicate about it with her teachers and school staff. Different children do need different care. Those who have a harder time walking need barriers removed for them. Those who cannot speak easily need lessons in how to manage it better. Those whose emotions are volatile need a safe place to express and release. That is how we care for them. That is how we love them. But to see them always as whole and complete in their humanity is to see the truth about them. And only in the truth are there no limits to how they can grow and learn and express what is most powerful and amazing in themselves. And it's only in the deep-rooted knowledge of their wholeness that they can have the courage to bring their love out into the world and teach everyone how to see them as whole. ♥

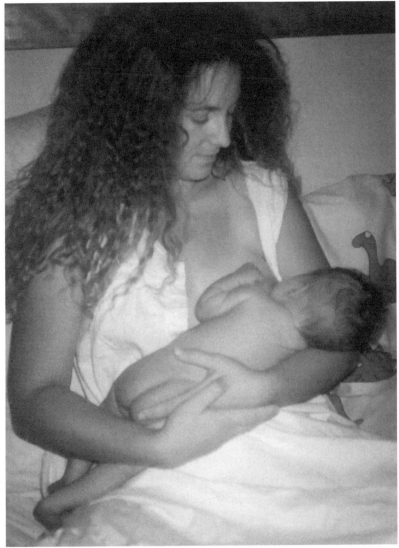

photo courtesy of David Murray and Dominique Brousseau

Why Your Baby
Loves to Be Touched

BY JODY WRIGHT

When I teach infant massage workshops, I ask parents and future instructors to share an experience of touch that was meaningful to them. One recalled when she was a teenager in the hospital and her mother stroked her forehead. Another mentioned her grandmother fixing her hair and how wonderful it felt. A third tearfully shared that touch was taboo in her family and remembered her unfulfilled yearning for it. A father described stroking his wife's back during labor and watching her relax.

Each of us has memories of touch, or the painful lack of it, in our lives. Why is it so important to us?

Before birth babies live in an environment of constant contact. As they grow, the space becomes tighter and tighter and the body contact more intense. Then comes birth, with a whole body massage as the baby is pushed through the birth canal, hopefully into a pair of loving hands.

This birth massage is an important part of preparing the intestines and lungs for their new functions. It replaces the licking that other mammals instinctively use to start these functions. Is it any surprise that after birth a baby feels most content in his mother's arms or lying on her chest?

In the hospital, the transfer to an bassinet is surely a "cold" experience. Studies have shown that full-term babies keep their temperature best when they are held close to their mothers after birth, with warmed blankets over them and caps on their heads. After all, mom is just the temperature they're used to! Your warmth will continue to be a reason your baby wants to touch you. He'll want to snuggle with you on a cold night, or gradually get used to the air temperature by being held in your lap after a bath or a nap.

Sleeping with your baby fulfills his need to be touched and helps him regulate his breathing. There are theories that this lowers the risk of Sudden Infant Death Syndrome. When you sleep with your baby it is easy to put out a hand and reassure him or to pull him toward you for a nurse in the dark.

I remember the first few weeks with one of my babies. She loved sleeping tucked under my arm. After a night or two I was able to turn my back to her without her waking, so I could curl up in my usual way. Then I would sneak away in the morning and leave my warm, mama-scented nightgown for her to snuggle up to while I showered. Gradually, she learned to sleep happily, knowing I was nearby.

For nine months your baby rose with you in the morning, accompanied you through your daily schedule, relaxed when you put your feet up, danced, exercised, and went to sleep with you. A baby carrier helps fulfill your baby's desire to remain close to you and participate in your day. A snuggly carrier that gives your baby a womb-like feeling is ideal for the first few months when warmth, closeness, and your gentle movement are what she really wants.

Studies have shown that babies who are carried more cry less and are more content. If you have a fussy one, try arranging your life for a little while so she can nap with you as you read a good book, and carry her around in a carrier as much as you can during the day.

Instinctively, an infant knows that his best assurance of survival is having a devoted parent near. Keeping in touch, whether at night or during the day, reassures him that all is well. Taking baths with your baby, letting him nap skin to skin on your chest, and massaging him will make you both feel close.

Touch, more than any other sense, is tied to our emotions. We feel intimate with those we touch. A new mother unwraps her baby as soon as she is alone with her and looks over every part of her body, counting her toes, memorizing her features. She touches first with tentative fingertips, and then with her full palm. She wants to see and feel that everything is right with her baby.

It seems that children have an "empty tank" sometimes, and they need to be reassured that they are loved and wanted. Touch is one of the best ways to fill this tank. When I was working long hours, leaving sixteen-month-old Emily home with Dad, I found her clingy when I got home. A rolling, hugging, nursing, playing session on the big bed was an ideal way for us to reconnect after a day apart. With her tank filled, she was happy to play while I cooked dinner.

Not only do we make our babies happier when we touch them, but they make us happier, too. Touching causes hormonal changes in our own bodies that make our hearts more open and our parenting easier. ♥

photo courtesy of Fern Reiss

photo courtesy of Laura Lambert

Take a Bath with Your Baby

BY ZIPORAH HILDEBRANDT

The first nine months of life are spent in a private tropical sea: warm, wet, dark, enclosed by a mother's flesh. Birth is entry into a world of air, light, and solids. The bath, in a way, is a return to that watery world.

Warm water is comforting to infants and babies. A bath can calm a fussy baby, nip a colic attack in the bud, and soothe a tired child right to sleep. Skin-to-skin contact with Mom or Dad strengthens the bond a baby depends on. Some babies dislike being completely undressed, and holding them chest-to-chest while slowly sinking into the bath can help them accept nakedness.

Taking your baby into the bath with you is usually easier than giving him a bath by himself. You know the water isn't too hot or too cold, because you're in it. You can wash with both hands by raising your knees and propping your baby on your thighs. And when one parent is bathing with the baby, the other can prepare a meal or take a break.

The key to success is to place an infant seat by the tub in a warm (80–85 degree) bathroom. Undress, and make sure you have everything you need for your bath, including an extra towel or a few washcloths to keep your wet baby warm. Place your baby on a towel in the infant seat, then sit in the tub and bring your baby in. Wash and play with her first. When you are ready to wash yourself, put her back in the seat and wrap the dry towel around her.

You can hold her head on your lap in the water, letting her body float between your legs. Sing her songs, play counting games, let her play with the water, give her a massage (don't use oil though, she'll get too slippery). There's no need for soap; it will make her difficult to hold, and it will dry out her skin too much.

You can shower with a infant, too, if you're confident in your ability to hold a slippery, squirming baby. It's a great way to give a baby a quick wash, if someone can hand him in to you and take him back when he's clean.

Bathing together can be an enjoyable family activity. As you take baths together through the years, you'll find new games, make up new songs, and maintain your close bond, long after the nursing years are over. ♥

photo courtesy of Diana Norman

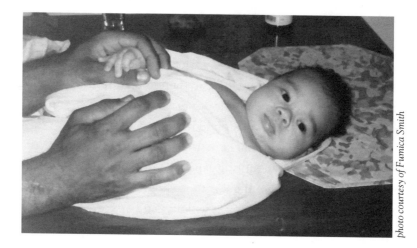

photo courtesy of Fumica Smith

Want to Massage Your Baby?
Just Do It!

BY JODY WRIGHT

From Russia to India to Africa, mothers and fathers have been massaging their babies for as long as anyone knows. All you need to get started is some unscented vegetable or nut oil, a towel and a pillow, and a warm, comfortable place to sit (the floor works well).

Undress your baby and lay him on the towel. Leave his shirt on if it is cool, or let him wiggle free. Use the pillow under your baby or to prop the back and head of your toddler.

Start by asking your baby's permission to massage her. This first time your baby won't know what you are asking, but next time she will. If your baby is willing, put a little oil on your hands and rub them together.

Massage your baby's legs and feet, using long strokes down the legs and feet first and concentrating on small places like ankles and toes afterward. Massage back up the leg and do clockwise strokes on the belly. Massage out from the middle of the chest, then down the arms. Sing a song to your baby or recite a little rhyme as you massage each finger. Carefully stroke her face, and then turn her over and massage her back. If she's still awake, she probably won't be much longer! ♥

Infant Massage:
A Way to Show You Care

BY JODY WRIGHT

Every evening from about six to eight, two-month-old Joshua had a fussy period. It wasn't really long and terrible, but it was a hard time for the whole family. Within a week or two of learning to massage her baby, Lori found that his fussy period rapidly diminished. Perhaps he was just growing out of it, she thought—until she missed doing his daily massage and his fussiness returned.

Denise was a La Leche League leader who had lots of experience with babies. But when her fourth was born with low muscle tone, didn't gain weight, and was fussy, she felt she needed more tools to help. The infant massage she learned was particularly helpful. "I found a new height of motherly peace and joy in what you taught me! THANK YOU!"

Jani was born seven weeks early and then passed around for two months until she was connected with her adoptive mother. When her new mother first saw her, she weighed about five pounds, remained curled up when unswaddled, and had scaly, dull skin. After a week of massage, it seemed Jani had discovered her whole body. She wiggled and stretched and her skin had a healthy glow. She began to gain weight and learned to respond to her mother's loving touch. She showed no lag in her development as a result of her prematurity.

Baby massage is a warm, loving way to improve a baby's physical and emotional well-being. Physically, it helps to strengthen and regulate a baby's respiratory and gastrointestinal functions. Problems such as colic can often be relieved with just a few weeks of daily massage, by helping the baby relax and increasing circulation.

Emotionally, it is an easy way for parents to fill their baby's need for touch, complete attention, and eye contact, at the same time fulfilling their own need for positive response from their baby. The parent who massages his or her baby finds

Motherwear photo

that the bond between the two of them becomes stronger, their ability to communicate with each other increases, and nurturing the baby becomes much easier.

A typical massage lasts about twenty minutes. A natural oil is used to reduce friction as the parent gives a smooth, flowing massage designed to relax the baby at the same time as it stimulates the circulation of blood. The parent often sings, talks lovingly, or tells stories and nursery rhymes as she or he massages.

Infant massage has been practiced by cultures all over the world. What a loving way for parents to connect with their babies! ♥

Babies Love Sounds

BY ZIPORAH HILDEBRANDT

Even before birth, sound fills the mind of a child. Digestive rumblings, mother's heartbeat, voices and music. Hearing is the most developed and precise of the senses at birth, so it is no wonder that infants are so sensitized to sound. It is also the most familiar in a world of strangeness. Light, cold, air—even the sensation of being touched, skin to skin, consciously, is totally new.

In a world buzzing with sound, our brains quickly screen out the repetitive, harmless and uninteresting. But what is boring and familiar to us is brand new to a baby. Babies tune in to the new, the subtle, the exciting. A truck going by is an event to the ear of an infant. The first time your baby associates your refrigerator with the sound it makes, she's likely to want to show you.

Young children are fascinated by the non-human creatures sharing our planet. Even in a city there are plenty of animals to listen for: dogs and cats, pigeons and sparrows, gulls, crickets, horses. What's that sound you didn't even notice until she called your attention to it? "Oh, a dog. No, we can't see the dog. The dog is barking." Listening for and imitating sounds is a game you can play together. A game that will draw you into your baby's unique world.

Avoid the "Cock-a-doodle-doo" syndrome. Listen for the sounds animals *really* make. "Quack" and "oink" are conventionalized names for animal sounds; the true sounds are much more interesting. And don't forget making up your own sounds! Babies love to create new sounds that get both of you giggling.

My daughter's first favorite book was a board book with a bright picture of one animal on each page. We made the sounds together as we turned the pages. Now, at five, she's answering the mourning doves and crows.

The world is full of fascination for our ears if we stop and listen. Leaves rustle in the breeze, snow hisses on the windowpanes, the toaster hums, the bubbles in the bath sigh as they collapse. Most of all, though, babies love to make sounds themselves. I have seen many babies enchanted by a crinkly cellophane wrapper instead of the cute toy packaged inside. Babies like to twang rubber bands and doorstops, throw things, bang things, flush toilets, slam doors, scream, and produce sounds in a myriad of ways. Unfortunately, their choice of methods are often destructive or irritating to others. With a little thought, however, your child's delight in sounds can be fostered with your sanity intact.

Offer your child choices. Instead of whacking the pot with a metal spoon, how about a wooden spoon? Maybe she could do it in another room. Maybe a plastic pail could substitute for the pot. Or an equally interesting but totally different sound, like tearing paper, might capture her attention.

Sound-producing toys flood the market. Talking books, talking dolls, all reflect the manufacturers' awareness of children's love of sounds. There are inexpensive electric keyboards that can produce the sounds of a dozen instruments. But there is a wealth of sound in the world free for the listening, and there's rich ground to plant the seeds of knowledge. More important, by attuning yourself to your baby and her interests, you create and nurture a bond she can grow on. Your interest tells her you respect her and value her awareness, building a foundation for self-esteem. ♥

photo courtesy of Elisabeth Liebow

"And Then What Happened?" Telling Stories to Children

BY ZIPORAH HILDEBRANDT

As we move through life, we are always telling stories and hearing them from others. "How was your day?" is the beginning of a story. Each of us is more chock-full of stories than a grandmother's cookie jar is of cookies.

From our very first memories, to the dreams we wish would come true, to flights of pure fancy, we are each capable of telling our stories. You probably tell stories already, without realizing they are stories.

Even before birth, your baby listens for the sound of your voice. After birth, it is one of the few familiar stimuli in her environment. She follows you with her ears as she follows you with her eyes. As an instrument, the human voice is marvelous, no two exactly alike, conveying emotion and recognition in the most subtle of variations. What better way of bonding than to tell the story of your love as you count your newborn's fingers or trace the delicate whorls of his ear? How better to maximize language acquisition than to tell the story of every moment as it happens to your wide-open audience? "Now I'm putting the saucers away, now I'm watering the African violets . . . ."

"Ah, but those aren't real stories," you might say. "I can't tell real stories." Think again. Every time you say, "When I was a little girl," or "Before you were born," you are telling a story.

I began telling my daughter stories about my own life when she reminded me of forgotten times. Then I began making up stories out of desperation, when I'd find myself in a situation without books or toys or other ways to occupy her. Like singing, telling stories is something you can do in the dark, in the car, on a hike. "Tell me a story," she has demanded since before she was three. When I pause to pour her juice or am distracted by a thought of my own, she says, "Read!" She finds no distinction between the stories I read from a book and the stories that emerge from

photo courtesy of Katrina Hill

my mouth as unplanned surprises.

Families throughout the world have told stories since before recorded history. Myths and legends, fairy tales and family doings. The distinctions blur after a few thousand years, just as they blur in the minds of the very young. "Are mermaids real?"

"And *then* what happened?" My daughter asks me this whenever I stop, even at what I thought was the end. "That's the end of the story," is unacceptable. I have to think of other ways to get out of it. "Then they all went to sleep and they won't wake up until tomorrow." Whether it's the time the basement flooded or Samantha the flying teddy bear's birthday, it is the continuity, the sense that the story goes on just as we do, that a child craves.

Your baby may be too young to talk or to appreciate the imaginative resources you find yourself tapping into. One of the beauties, and joys, of telling stories is that it doesn't matter. You're creating special moments with her. Car rides, waiting rooms and check-out lines become opportunities, especially if you have older siblings. How better to captivate a littlest one than with the sight of the adored older sibling listening raptly to your words?

How do you start? With something familiar. A favorite toy engaged in a familiar situation is often enough. If you're washing the dishes or doing the laundry, make that the start of the story. What a delightful experience to give outlet to your own boredom with routine! Send Peter the stuffed tiger on an imaginary journey through the back of the washing machine. Look around for inspiration. In the land behind the washing machine, perhaps trees grow sneakers. Let your eye travel over the objects in the room. Your imagination will get into gear.

Or, you can start with a story you already know, even one you don't remember well, and change it. Maybe Cinderella would rather have a horse than a prince. The three little pigs could start a rock band instead of building houses. Don't worry about plot. Your child doesn't care, because it's your story. In fact, the sillier the better.

Sometimes you will feel too rooted in the real world for flights of fantasy. Then you can draw on your own memories. Losing your first tooth, how you felt about your hair, a favorite game or toy, a visit to relatives, stories about siblings and parents, what you did for holidays—all are wonderful subjects to share. And you'll be passing on a wealth of family history and real-life experience along with the entertainment.

You and your child may develop favorite characters you'll go back to again and again. My daughter loves the "Cranky Family," which includes forgetful parents, selfish older siblings, and a precocious baby who loves garlic and talks to badgers. But the important thing is the telling, not the story itself. It's the telling that strengthens the bond between you and your child, a bond that reaches back to the beginnings of consciousness and will last your child's whole life. And who knows, maybe some of your stories will be told to your children's children, and to their children. ♥

photo courtesy of Jody Wright

The Most Perfect Baby
in the Whole Wide World

BY JODY WRIGHT

I'll bet you're the one—the one with "The Most Perfect Baby in the Whole Wide World." Oh, I know, after last night you probably aren't sure, but aren't there times when you feel that way? I know I do. At various moments, sometimes in the same day, I tell each of my daughters, "You're the most wonderful daughter in the world." And at that moment, I feel that way, with no duplicity. It is really a heart feeling, and doesn't have anything to do with logic.

Have you ever looked back at a photo you adored of one of your children and realized he wasn't really quite as cute as you thought back then? Have you seen another parent gaze adoringly at a rather humble-looking child, as you felt glad YOUR child looked the way she did? Or how about the new parent who suddenly discovers the joys of parenting, and acts as if she or he has just discovered something no one else knew about: the well-kept secret that you can fall as head over heels in love with a child as you can with an adult? (No one sings about it on the radio.)

I remember watching my next door neighbor fall in love with his child. Toward the eighth month of his wife's pregnancy, he came to a childbirth class at my house with a new interest in what was being said. The financial fears that fathers face early in pregnancy had given way to a sudden realization that this baby was coming soon! Excitement started to build in his eyes, along with a growing sense of responsibility and caring. Then, when the baby came, he was so proud to show her off, so pleased to be the one she slept on. Life changed completely and a new world opened up for him. It was like looking at everything from a completely different point of view.

Parents aren't the only ones who fall in love. I've found that each time we have a new baby in our family, everyone rallies around. After the initial shifts in roles are ironed out, a new harmony comes into the family, with the baby as the nucleus of the circle.

When we adopted our last child, Liina (who had been our youngest) was very worried about the role change it would mean for her. She had spent six years in the privileged youngest role and knew Mom would now be busy with the baby. I asked her how she felt after Emily arrived. "I had no idea she would be so cute!" she told me. "I fell in love with her as soon as I saw her."

When I hear parents brag about their children, or show off pictures, I smile because I know that means everything is going just fine. Someone fell in love with that child, and lost all perspective. All they see is "The Most Perfect Baby in the Whole Wide World." Doesn't every baby deserve to be the most perfect baby to someone? I wish every child in the world could have just that. ♥

CHAPTER TWO

Motherwear photo

Breastfeeding

Breastfeeding is the epitome of nurturing, as a mother sustains her baby with our species' most perfect food. It marks a unique and precious time in the lives of a mother and child: a time, while relatively short-lived, that sets the stage for their long-term relationship and all others to come. Breastfeeding is good for our babies, good for us, good for our society, and good for our planet.

Nursing isn't always easy in today's fast-paced world. Women need both commitment and support to succeed. Motherwear is dedicated to all of the values that breastfeeding inspires: healthy mothers and babies, a nurturing parent-child bond, and faith in our hearts to know what is best for us, our children, and our families.

photo courtesy of Trish Ruppel

The Magic of Milk

BY BETH HERSH

There is a substance flowing in the bodies of nursing mothers. It is pure, wholesome, and nourishing. It is always available, at the perfect temperature. It is in endless supply, because even as it flows it is being replenished. Used worldwide to completely nourish infants, it provides immunity to many diseases. It supplies protein, vitamins, minerals, fats, carbohydrates, and water. It helps restless babies fall asleep and grouchy babies wake up.

Is it magic? You might say so. Mother's milk, both by its content and by the act of nursing, is the most complete system of nurturing we can give our babies. It is a living substance that is always changing to be exactly what they need.

Our milk is different at the beginning of each feeding. When the baby is most hungry it contains more protein and water, more substance. Minutes later, when the baby is relaxed, it has an increased fat content so it will be digested more slowly. The flavor varies according to what we mothers eat. If spicy burritos are a family treat, the nursling will develop a taste for them before she even sits at the table.

First milk, or colostrum, is power-packed with protein and immunity factors. It then changes to become whatever the individual baby needs. Studies have shown that the breastmilk from mothers of premature babies is markedly different than the milk of full-term babies' mothers. The milk for infants is different from that for toddlers, for whom it is only a supplement.

What is most amazing to me—our milk is filled with an ever-changing array of antibodies to help fight off whatever virus the baby has come in contact with. Whenever a virus enters a mother's system, she immediately starts producing antibodies to counteract it. These antibodies go into her milk, so her baby has some protection from the cold or flu she is carrying. What is even more incredible is that if a baby picks up a virus, she will transfer it from her mouth to the breast. Then the breast will begin to produce the antibodies she needs. This may be the only cure for the common cold!

photo courtesy of Valentine Christian

Aside from the substance of the milk, there is quite a bit of magic in the act of nursing. Picture this: you're at a wedding and the bride is just starting down the aisle. You turn to catch her radiance, and suddenly the baby in your arms starts to fuss. Discreetly, you move your blouse and tuck the baby in. In one easy motion you are meeting his emotional as well as his physical needs. People are unaware that there is a baby there, let alone one that is nursing. He's happy, you're happy; it's a magic moment all around! ♥

Why Is Breastfeeding So Important?

BY JODY WRIGHT

In the early 1980s, 61 percent of mothers leaving hospitals with their newborn babies had begun breastfeeding. That number has already dropped by more than 7 percent. In a time when the benefits of breastfeeding are so well publicized, we're left to wonder: Why?

Breastfeeding helps form a loving bond.

Touch, smell, skin and eye contact, and even the hormones involved in nursing are the things that make us fall in love with our children and that help them learn to love and trust us. Much of the crime, drug use, and insensitivity that have become characteristic of this decade may be due in part to the lack of a strong primary bond that accompanies breastfeeding and other nurturing behaviors. People who grow up feeling uncertain about love and acceptance have trouble developing sensitivity and caring for others.

Our high rate of divorce indicates to me that a lot of people lacked the first loving relationship that would have taught them how to be intimate, trusting, and sharing with others. How fortunate that many of us get another chance: Developing a close bond with one's own child is a way for adults from rocky childhoods to begin unraveling their pain.

Breastfeeding improves a child's health.

Studies comparing breastfed and formula-fed infants have shown that breastfeeding reduces respiratory and gastrointestinal illnesses through immunity factors and digestive aids passed from mother to child. Formula feeding increases the rate of severe liver disease, diabetes, cancer, and many other diseases later in life.

Part of this is due to breastmilk's composition. Made from a mother's blood, it has the exact vitamins and minerals a child needs, in the forms in which they are most easily assimilated by humans. Milk is filled with nutrients and immunity factors that have yet to be identified or replicated. The nutritional and immuno-logic composition of the milk is adjusted for the age of the child, the time of day, the

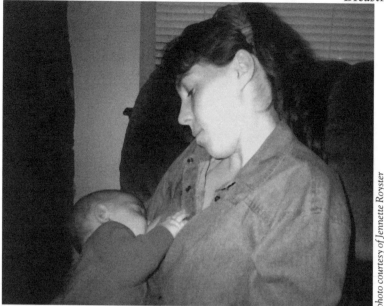

photo courtesy of Jennette Royster

length of the nursing, and the illnesses to which the mother and/or child have been exposed. As a bonus, it is always fresh.

Allergies have become increasingly prevalent over the years. People are exposed to so many more substances today than in the past: foods that come from around the world, new pesticides and fertilizers, manufactured materials of questionable composition. And with the decline in breastfeeding, children's defenses against allergies are weakened. Breastfeeding, even for a short period, has been clearly associated with a lower incidence of wheezing, prolonged colds, diarrhea, and vomiting. It seems that with all the new substances and pollutants our children will be exposed to in the 21st century, the benefits of breastfeeding's allergy protection are vital.

Breastfeeding is good for Mom, too.

It isn't just the baby who benefits when a mother decides to nurse. Mom does, too. The closeness of bonding, relaxation from the hormones of breastfeeding, and the ease of parenting a healthier child are all wonderful byproducts. In addition, the mother who breastfeeds finds that her body returns to normal more quickly and she loses weight more easily. Over the years this natural completion of the cycle of birth seems to reduce breast cancer and possibly other diseases of the female system.

In this fast-changing world there are so many things we as individuals cannot control. When it comes to our own children, though, there is plenty we can do. Giving them a healthy, loving start can make a world of difference to their future and to the future of the human race. When mothers start out breastfeeding, children get the best start there is. ♥

The Message Is Love

BY BETH HERSH

Why do babies suddenly have a desire to nurse at what seems to be the worst possible moment? Are they really hungry? What is this need that nursing satisfies so well?

Babies need to know they are loved. This is a need so vital that without it they would die. They could have the very best of food and 24-hour professional care, but unless they feel they are loved, they cannot survive.

How easy it would be if we could just let go of what people might think and nurse our babies wherever we are. In one easy motion we would be meeting her emotional and her physical needs, to say nothing of the peace of mind it would bring to us to have a moment of quiet in the midst of chaos.

How do we transmit this essential message to our babies? The first way is to hold them a lot. Warmth and comfort as they snuggle gives them physical security. Then we talk to them; make contact. When they meet our eyes and hear our voices, they know they are being recognized. When they reach out with a coo or a smile, we respond. That is how they know they exist.

Breastfeeding easily fulfills all these needs as well as the need for good nutrition. Babies nurse in the warm comfort of our embrace, and this is where they usually begin their first communication with us. As I sit here typing, I have a picture in my mind of my little five-month-old Zoe in my arms, nursing herself to sleep. She starts by squirming around to the best position. Then she pops off once or twice to look at me to see if I'm ready to play. With a big smile she goes back to nursing while keeping an eye on me. She's still smiling as the nipple falls out of her mouth. Then with a sigh and a snuggle, she settles in for some serious nursing.

Within seconds, she is fast asleep. I shift a bit in my chair and she lets go. She is completely relaxed. The last trickle of milk escapes her mouth and rolls down her chin. Is our milk magic? I think it is. Is the message Love? Most definitely. ♥

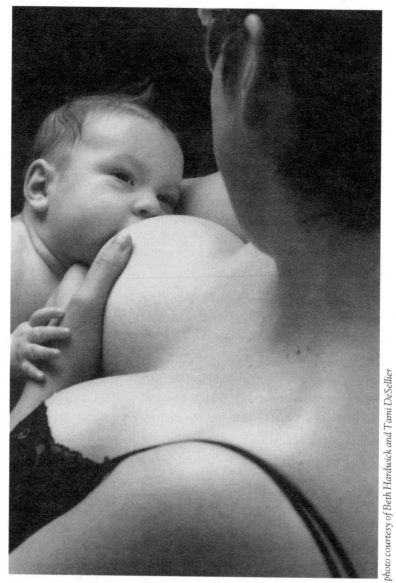

photo courtesy of Beth Hardwick and Tami DeSellier

The Elements of
Breastfeeding Success

BY JODY WRIGHT

Succeeding at nursing is not only important for our babies, it is important for us, too. We feel good when we have been offered a challenge and succeed at it. Here are some ideas drawn from my own experience of nursing four babies and counseling others as a La Leche League leader.

Learn as much as you can before your baby arrives.

Talking to knowledgeable people and educating yourself are some of the most important things you can do to help ensure success at breastfeeding. Choose a few good books on breastfeeding and read them while you are pregnant. Don't just borrow favorites; have them nearby for easy reference later when you have a concern.

Attend a support group.

Women used to learn breastfeeding by watching the mothers around them. Perhaps they also remembered what nursing was like when they were toddlers themselves. They watched their siblings, cousins, and neighbors nurse. Modern parenting is often more isolating. Give yourself a chance to see experienced mothers nurse, get answers to your questions, and establish links for support if you need it. Expectant mothers who attend La Leche League meetings or other support groups are much more likely to breastfeed their babies easily and for as long as they choose.

Have a prepared birth with as little interference as possible.

When you educate yourself about birth, make a clear birth plan, and choose attendants carefully, you are more likely to have a natural birth or one with few unexpected interventions. This will allow both you and your baby to be alert and healthy and will give you both a good start with breastfeeding.

Breastfeed as soon as possible after birth.

Studies have shown that babies seem to have a natural interest in nursing soon after birth. Babies able to nurse at this time seem to catch on better. Continue to nurse often in the first few days, even if your baby doesn't appear to be getting much. Nursing early and often will decrease the amount of engorgement you experience, allow your baby to learn to nurse well before lots of milk comes in, and give your baby the colostrum that is filled with the immunity factors, nutrients, and natural laxatives your baby needs at this time.

Keep your baby with you.

Nursing isn't just a way to feed but a way to parent. Keeping your baby with you in the hospital will improve communications between you. Spending the first few weeks after birth together will help you recover from the birthing process and will help unite you both in a way you may never have imagined.

Listen to your baby and feed her when she tells you it is time.

As your baby gets older, try to arrange your life so it is easy to stay together. Set priorities. Hold off our culture's pressures to return to a job and separate from your baby. This is a once-in-a-lifetime chance for both of you. Do your best to utilize it.

Avoid pacifiers and bottles.

Don't confuse your baby. Learning to nurse is challenging. Other ways of sucking make it hard for babies to master nursing. Pacifiers and bottles added an extra two months to the time it took one of my babies to become skilled at nursing. Even under ideal circumstances, it isn't unusual for it to take several months for a baby to become a nursing expert. Adding pacifiers or bottles makes it more difficult.

Cultivate friendships and support from other nursing mothers.

Having friends and acquaintances who nurse will give you support if you run into problems. You'll have more viewpoints to draw from if someone says you should be weaning your baby. You'll have access to others' experiences with doctors, and you'll know you aren't alone when parenting gets rough. Your La Leche League or support group, along with your childbirth preparation class, are good places to meet people.

If you have problems, get help. Check your hospital, midwife, HMO, or pediatrician for a referral, or call your La Leche League leader for advice and a listening ear. It is easy in the stressful months after birth to give up when nursing doesn't go as you planned. It may take a little more work, be a little harder, or not be exactly what you expected. Your own determination to find an answer and to try something new becomes the major factor if things aren't going right with nursing.

Stick to it, find the help you need, be determined, and you'll probably be able to solve the problem. ♥

photo courtesy of Laura Lambert

Mothers Share: Our readers discuss
The Challenges of Nursing

COMPILED BY JODY WRIGHT

We were all first-time parents once, floundering to cope with tasks and skills we were just beginning to learn. We read books, talked to our families and friends, and gradually figured out how to get through the difficult times.

When we asked our readers about the challenges of nursing, one problem came up again and again—lack of support. Nursing mothers face the disapproval of family, in-laws, friends, health care providers, community members, and most of all, the general public. As babies pass their first twelve months, many mothers commented, the pressure to wean begins to mount, even from formerly supportive husbands and relatives.

Although lack of support is frustrating and painful for many women, respondents strongly agreed that they would continue to breastfeed, because they felt it was the best thing for them and their babies. Only one woman who responded had just given up. She wrote, "I regret it so much . . . . Get the support from anyone, and take your time. Don't give in like me—please! I'm now giving my baby gross formula which is expensive. It stains clothing and is a pain to prepare with a crying baby in the next room."

Mothers Share asked: "What is the biggest problem you have encountered as a breastfeeding mom?"

Support

"The biggest problem I encountered as a nursing mother was getting support. I had support from my husband and family, but I lacked support from my friends who had babies, but chose to bottle feed. I am the only one who chose to breastfeed, and I feel like a minority. (There is no local La Leche group—but should be!) I guess I miss just having someone to talk to, get advice. I keep telling myself that I am doing what is best for my son, and I love the close contact that breastfeeding has given us. I will continue to breastfeed my son until he decides to wean himself!"

"My biggest problem is dealing with not being in the cultural norm. The way to deal with it is just to keep on nursing in public until they get used to us—and learn by our example."

"The biggest problem I encountered was the 'baby looks hungry . . . sounds hungry . . . is hungry' syndrome. My parents didn't support my decision to breastfeed. They didn't see how a 'tiny little thing' like me could feed a hungry baby. Things really took off when I delivered an almost-ten-pound baby. Whenever she would cry, they would tell me it was a hungry cry and pressure me to add cereal to her diet. Finally I bought a box of cereal, but after feeding it to her twice, I realized my baby was doing great on breastmilk and chucked the cereal. A breastfeeding mother learns to trust herself."

"My family expects me to put my baby on a bottle so they can baby-sit. It's still unresolved."

"The nurses at the hospital weren't too helpful, and I had a hard time positioning the baby, so I had to rent a video to learn the correct positioning. The pediatrician was telling me to give Eric one bottle a day starting when he was two weeks old—which I didn't do. Now he's more supportive of my exclusive nursing, since, at four and a half months, Eric is seventeen pounds and thriving! But he's my first baby, and deciding to ignore a doctor's orders was a little scary."

"My biggest ongoing problem has been my fear of nursing my son in public. At first I only took him out right after he'd eaten and would get back home well before he got hungry again. I did this for a long time because I'm really shy about it. However, I'm finally overcoming this."

"My biggest problem was with neonatal intensive care doctors. My son was born two months early and spent his first precious month of life in the hospital. I was told not to nurse him and that he would go home sooner if he took a bottle. I insisted he only be given my milk. (I produced a rich yellow milk containing colostrum until he was forty-one weeks gestational age!) With the help of a lactation specialist I spent the second month of his life teaching him to nurse. My son was two months old when he really started nursing and is now a happy, healthy, nursing, eighteen-month-old toddler."

Leaking

"Leaking while nursing has been a constant problem. Now I either put a folded-up washcloth in my bra while nursing or I put a sterilized bottle up to my breast to catch the milk. Then dad can use the bottle to feed the baby later on."

"I have flat nipples but didn't realize it until after my baby was born. Consequently, I wear breast shields between feedings, and my breast problem is major-league leaking. I have tried many combinations of washable and disposable breast pads, but the only thing that really keeps me dry is folded diapers in my bra. At a time when feeling attractive is often elusive, diapers do little to help."

Nipple Confusion

"My problem was with nipple confusion at one week old and at three months old. We quit giving our baby the supplemental bottle. When she got hungry enough she took the breast (had to wait six hours). It's most important to understand that the problem isn't you—don't blame yourself. Stay relaxed."

Painful Nursing

"When my first child was born I found breastfeeding very painful. Nothing seemed to help. Then, magically about four weeks later, the pain disappeared. Just wait it out. It's really worth it!"

"I got mastitis—an incredibly painful breast infection resulting from badly plugged ducts. Fortunately my LLL leader recommended warm, moist compresses on the inflamed area, and my physician prescribed an antibiotic compatible with breastfeeding. With this regimen, the infection cleared up completely and I didn't have to stop nursing my son, even temporarily."

"Baby biting. I don't want to respond too negatively, yet when the baby bites my breast with her razor-sharp teeth it sends me though the roof."

"The third day my nipples blistered. Some babies are born with a tendency to bite while sucking. Things I have tried are vitamin E oil [on nipples] just after feeding; my own milk rubbed on the nipples; exposure to air for at least fifteen minutes after feeding; gently chanting "Easy, baby, easy"; most effectively, gently massaging the area just in front of the ear but behind the cheek, so as not to confuse her rooting response (taught to me by a professional singer)."

Sore Nipples

"Vitamin E was my lifesaver—the problem cleared up in just one day!"

". . . copious use of lanolin and Unpetroleum Jelly coupled with a hair dryer used on the nipples as often as I could—five minutes every two hours at first."

"I finally had to stop nursing my first child because she developed thrush, and my nipples got so sore I was crying each time I nursed. I dreaded each feeding. I was not in touch with La Leche League, and my pediatrician was ill-informed. She just had me treat my daughter's mouth, not my nipples, so we kept passing the fungus back and forth. This is a painful memory for me, emotionally."

"I got incredible, sharp pains within the nipples and breasts within the first two days. A call to my homeopathic physician and two doses of a remedy cleared it right up!"

Vaginal Dryness

"The biggest problem has been extreme vaginal dryness associated with breastfeeding. Believe me, we've tried everything to help make intercourse more comfortable. I don't want to quit nursing, so the problem is not quite resolved."

Attachment

"I've not been able to leave my daughter for more than three or four hours at a time. She will not take a bottle at all. Now, at six months old, she is so attached to me it's even hard to leave the room without her getting upset. I don't want to force weaning on her, because I want her to get the benefits of mother's milk. I feel caught, torn, and confused."

Lack of Appetite

"My biggest problem was with our seventh baby, who was born naturally at home after six cesareans. She was such a contented baby, she didn't nurse much the first several days. Having never cared for a baby the first twenty-four hours, I didn't think of waking her. Eventually she quit wetting her diapers—and I wised up. What a scare she gave. I just thank God we didn't lose her!"

Exhaustion

"My biggest problem both times was being too tired—I didn't get enough rest because I felt I had too much to do: cook, clean. Newborn-baby breastfeeding takes more time and patience." ♥

Motherwear photo

Lay a Strong Foundation
for Breastfeeding Success

BY ZIPORAH HILDEBRANDT

I feel very lucky to have breastfed my daughter as long as I wanted to—over four years. I see our nursing relationship as the foundation for the closeness we share now, three years later. We recreate that bond of love whenever we're together.

I see a long, successful breastfeeding relationship as the best and easiest way to establish that precious intimacy between mother and child. When I hear of moms who lacked the resources to continue nursing, I want to cry. "If only you had someone to call," I think sadly. "If only you had a book," and "If only you had the support you needed to trust your heart."

My heart goes out to all those women who gave up breastfeeding out of ignorance, bad advice, or lack of support. There are better solutions to those problems. It is very, very rare that a mom *must* stop breastfeeding. Here, then, are the foundation stones a woman can lay for herself so she will be equipped to overcome problems.

Read.

It can't be said enough. Read when you're pregnant, then read while you're nursing. Every problem I've heard of is mentioned in *The Womanly Art of Breastfeeding*, La Leche League International's invaluable reference.

Sore nipples, plugged ducts, infections in mothers, and poor weight gain in infants are often caused by incorrect positioning. *Bestfeeding: Getting Breastfeeding Right for You*, is a terrific resource and teaching aid for learning to nurse and getting positioning right.

These books are truly indispensable. If you read them—or whatever books you can find—cover to cover, you will likely end up knowing more about nursing than your doctor does! If you're reluctant to spend the money, look in your local library. If the library doesn't have them, request them through an interlibrary loan, or borrow books from a parenting or birthing library, a midwife, a childbirth educator, or a friend.

Contact La Leche League International.

Call 1-800-LA LECHE to find groups and leaders in your area. If there are none accessible to you, subscribe to LLLI's magazine, *New Beginnings.* Each issue is packed with information and warm, wonderful, encouraging support from other breastfeeding moms. LLLI also has a number of excellent booklets on many aspects of breastfeeding.

Establish a network of support.

Lack of support is the most common reason mothers give for abandoning nursing. It is very important to find the support you'll need as soon as possible, especially if people around you are disapproving.

Let the people in your life know how important breastfeeding is to you and your child. Your partner, family members, friends, and health providers are all potential sources of high quality support. Try to meet other breastfeeding moms, whether through a childbirth class, an LLL group, or just at the local park.

Many people will have concerns, even fears about breastfeeding. LLLI has literature designed specifically for this purpose. Misconceptions can be cleared up with accurate information.

People who care about you will also care about what's important to you. Seek out those around you who will support your decision to breastfeed because it's important to *you.* Find someone who will listen when a problem arises and help you keep going. Talk with someone who will encourage you to consult your books, call a lactation consultant, and remember why you chose to breastfeed in the first place.

Trust your heart. Trust yourself. Trust your baby.

When you're struggling with doubtful advice or disapproval, hold your baby close and feel the bond between you. It's the same bond that has guided mothers since the beginning of time. You and your baby have thousands of generations of wisdom holding you together. There is a way. It may be difficult for a time, but choosing nurturing over fear will strengthen your bond and make you a stronger mother and woman. And when your baby is a parent for the first time, he or she won't have to search for the support and knowledge that came with such effort to you, because you'll be there. ♥

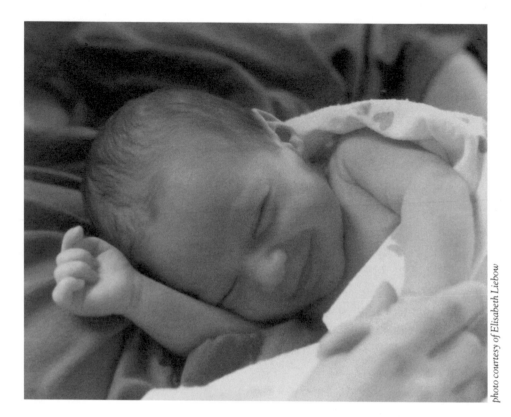

photo courtesy of Elisabeth Liebow

The Amazing Health Benefits
of Nursing

BY JODY WRIGHT

More and more studies are showing the amazing health benefits of nursing and how vital it is that infants be breastfed. One study found that the cost of hospital treatment for bottle-fed infants was fifteen times higher than that for breastfed babies. Studies done by UNICEF in Latin America and the Caribbean showed that infants who were breastfed for less than six months or not at all were six to fourteen times more likely to die in the second six months of life than those who were breastfed for six months or more.

Breastfed infants have lower rates of ear and respiratory infections, diarrheal illnesses, and atopic skin disorders than their bottle-fed counterparts. Exclusive breastfeeding has been shown to help prevent allergic disease in high-risk families. Better visual development and improved oral development have both been associated with breastfeeding.

In developing countries, breastfeeding is vital to the survival of children. It has been estimated that there are ten to twenty million young children with severe malnutrition at any one time, most of whom will die without treatment. In the English-speaking areas of the Caribbean, the hospital cost of malnutrition in young children, largely related to inadequate lactation, was calculated to be $10 million. According to UNICEF (*The State of the World's Children*, 1991), bottle-feeding causes the deaths of 1.5 million babies every year and ill health in countless others.

In the *Healthy People 2000* report, the U.S. Secretary of Health and Human Services set a goal "to increase to at least seventy-five percent the proportion of mothers who breastfeed their babies in the early postpartum period and to at least fifty percent the proportion who continue breastfeeding until their babies are five to six months old."

The benefits of breastfeeding affect the nursing mother as well. Nursing helps the uterus return to normal size after birth and helps a mother lose weight. Women who nurse their babies have a reduced chance of developing breast and ovarian cancers, and breastfeeding may provide protection against osteoporosis and hip fractures later in life.

The benefits to a child's emotional health are immeasurable, as the bond that results from breastfeeding sets the tone for a lifetime of relationships. In a world where families are spreading out and breaking up with frightening regularity, the importance of knowing how to form and foster good relationships is unquestioned. Healthy bodies, happy lives: the amazing benefits of breastfeeding. ♥

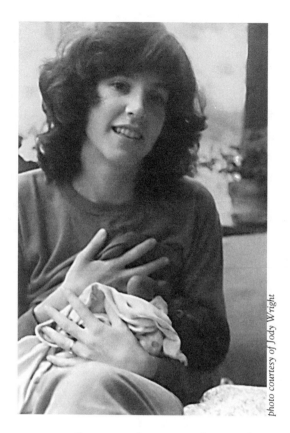

photo courtesy of Jody Wright

Nursing the Adopted Baby

BY JODY WRIGHT

Olisa was born at home just five hours before Prakash and I arrived at her mother's apartment. I sat most of the next day with her asleep in my lap, gazing into her eyes and imprinting her in my heart; taking complete responsibility for this little one who was going to be my first child. I also got a chance to try nursing in the four days we stayed there. It wasn't easy. Since I had never been pregnant, my nipples were soft and difficult for her to grasp. Like most new mothers, I felt clumsy. But Olisa took it all in stride.

I first read about nursing adopted babies in Tine Thevenin's book *The Family Bed*. I decided that if I ever adopted I was going to sleep with my baby and nurse her, too. So, in the months preparing for Olisa's arrival, I had researched adoptive nursing and, through La Leche League, met a mother who was nursing her eight-month-old adopted daughter. She taught me how to use a supplementer, which hung around my neck and had a flexible tube so Olisa could suck formula along with whatever milk my breast provided.

It took a few weeks for Olisa and me to get good at nursing, and I used a bottle to feed her some at first. I've heard that other mothers have used eye droppers or spoons until nursing was well established. It took only a little while for my nipples to begin to change into a shape more suitable for nursing. At first Olisa would whimper five or ten minutes into a feeding as she began to tire of all the work. Somehow she seemed to think that if she stopped, she couldn't get back on again, and she wasn't full yet! Once we got that straightened out and learned better ways of positioning ourselves, she would have nothing more to do with a bottle. She wanted her momma!

Next there was the world to conquer. Olisa is half African and half Filipino, so there was no way I could pass her off as my birth baby. I had to do a lot of explaining about breastfeeding her. I finally just decided I was an educational force, promoting nursing, and did my best to explain to people how important nursing was and how adoptive nursing works. People particularly wanted to know whether I was producing milk. I explained that nursing the baby caused hormonal changes so my body began to produce small amounts of milk. A similar process happens with birth mothers: the more they nurse, the more milk they produce. If they stop nursing, their milk dries up. A mother who has stopped nursing her baby and wants to resume may be able, with good guidance, to return to nursing using this same principle.

I soon recognized some of the hormonal changes that nursing mothers feel: a warm and serene feeling after a few minutes of nursing, an increased ability to deal with night wakings, an intense intuitive attachment to their babies. I love the "high" that nursing gives me; it helps me slow down to the pace of my babies.

Attending La Leche League meetings was important for all the questions I had. I really needed to meet monthly with a group of women who would tell me how wonderful it was that I was nursing Olisa. They gave me the energy I needed to keep going.

The quantity of milk I was producing was an issue for me. I really wanted to eliminate the supplementer, but my milk supply didn't increase enough. I never really knew how much milk I was producing, since there was no way to measure it. I could only watch the decreasing amount of supplement Olisa was taking. I tried taking herbs, nutritional yeast, etc., to increase my milk supply, but I finally had to change my idea of what was "successful." Success came to be the long, warm, nursing relationship we had developed together.

Looking back at nursing my four babies brings tears to my eyes. There is no doubt that I would do it again ten times over! When you nurse a baby, you don't just feed him milk, you feed him love. And when you nurse an adopted baby, it helps tie both of you into a biological process that has nurtured love and bonding in both mothers and babies for millions of years. ♥

Tandem Nursing

BY AMY MAGER

When I found myself expecting again as my son turned ten months old, I realized I had to make an important decision. Would I fully wean my son, who, at that time, was not very interested in food and loved to nurse, or would I begin to prepare for tandem nursing: breastfeeding two children? It didn't seem like much of a choice. I knew what felt right in my heart. What I needed was support for nursing both my babies.

I started to research the topic but found little information. I called a friend in Chicago who is wholeheartedly in favor of tandem nursing and participates in a tandem nursing moms' group. She, in turn, referred me to a mom who was nursing three children. These connections were most helpful.

I was surprised that I had more energy with my second pregnancy than I'd had with my first, even though I was nursing. My nipples got a little more sensitive, and I had to be conscious about good positioning on the breast. My son nursed more often for shorter periods. Changes in taste from mature milk to colostrum didn't seem to bother him.

Nursing can bring on labor at the end of the pregnancy, as the body's oxytocin levels increase to stimulate and continue contractions. Rashi nursed during labor and kept the process flowing smoothly. Emma was born after a six-hour labor next to our family bed.

Five minutes after Emma's birth, Rashi nursed as his sister rested on my chest. Before long, they were nursing together. Sometimes this was a wonderful experience for all of us. Other times it was too much, and alternatives had to be found.

Once the mature yummy milk came in, Rashi wanted to nurse more often. I had to define the limits of what I could lovingly handle, then communicate it clearly so he would understand. Nursing an older child and resenting it is in no one's best interest. Letting my son know that the baby needed to nurse first was a challenge in the beginning. Soon though, he understood that there was enough for

photo courtesy of Amy Mager and Jharna Morrisey

him too, and that they could nurse together.

The biggest demands of tandem nursing came in the first three months when both of my children were nursing like newborns. I was exhausted and could only nurse, eat, and rest or sleep. It is paramount to remember to eat and drink enough and to check with a health-care practitioner about taking a calcium/magnesium supplement, since it is very difficult to obtain as much calcium as you need through food at this time.

I never dreamed I would have problems with things like sore nipples with Emma, since I was already nursing. I was surprised by the depths of the challenges I found in breastfeeding during the first weeks. She developed thrush, which Rashi didn't get even though they both nursed often. I vigilantly followed my homeopath's instructions, using powdered food-grade charcoal and water on my nipples and in her mouth. I clearly understood why some people stop nursing when it gets really hard.

At first, some friends and family gave me a rough time about tandem nursing. This had more to do with the appropriateness of nursing a toddler than concerns for their health. But after they saw how both children bonded and thrived, their concerns waned. I was thankful for the support of my husband, my mother, my midwife, my homeopath, and Jody at Motherwear. Support is key to the success of tandem nursing. Doing what you know to be right and supportive of your family is essential. If there is room in your life to accommodate the extra demands on your body and spirit, tandem nursing can be an incredibly fulfilling experience. It makes you rest and be with your kids. And as an added benefit to moms, the prolactin released in the body during nursing is a relaxant! The rewards far outweigh the sacrifices.

Whenever Emma fusses now, Rashi tells me she needs some "nonny" (nursing). If he's nursing, he will come off the breast and tell me that it's Emma's turn. When they nurse together, Emma looks at her brother and reaches out to hold his hand. They learn to share everything, and know there is enough for both of them. I am told that children who nurse at the breast together maintain a special bond throughout life. I am very thankful to have a big chair with room for everyone. ♥

Mothers Share: Our readers discuss
Expressing Milk

COMPILED BY JODY WRIGHT

As a La Leche League leader, one of my most common counseling calls goes something like this: "Hi, I got your number from the La Leche League sheet at my doctor's office. I'm Janet New-Mom. My baby is six weeks old, and I'm going back to work next week. I've been trying to express milk, but I can't seem to get very much. Am I doing something wrong?"

I try to hide the fact that I myself have never conquered milk expression (mostly because I never needed to), and pull out my mental list of ways to help mothers express milk. "Most mothers find it takes some practice to learn how, just as it would to learn how to milk a cow. The key is to relax so you'll let down your milk."

Then I listen. Is the problem with the time of day she's trying? The technique? Is she having trouble relaxing? Does she really need to express milk, or is there a way she and her baby could get together during the work day? Is the homemaking mother wanting to express because *she* wants to go out or because her mother thinks she should be able to "get away"? All these pieces of information help me give the right suggestions to a new mom, but still I wish I had more personal experience to offer. [*Note: Some lactation specialists recommend starting pumping after six weeks in order to allow your milk supply to become more established.*]

Mothers Share asked: "If you have pumped your milk, what techniques have worked for you? Any hints for moms having trouble expressing?"

"Hand expressing is the quickest and least bothersome. Once when I was hospitalized for seven days I used an electric pump. That also worked fine. The hospital provided the sterile equipment and container. I find hand pumps useless!"

"I *love* my electric pump (both sides at once), which I have been fortunate enough to rent. I have not yet had to pump at work because I have managed to convince my employer to let me work at home half time."

"I've only used a cylinder-type pump and have had no problem. I have an easier time pumping in the morning. I seem to have more milk then—so much more that my baby is satisfied nursing on one side and I pump the other."

"I did quite a bit of pumping with my first, when I was in graduate school. I was able to do this at home, then freeze the milk to be given to my son while I was at class. The best advice I was given was to express just *before* a feeding. The best time of all is early morning (assuming you've had a decent night's sleep.)"

"I've never had much luck, but now that my first born is thirteen and a half, I cherish even more the nursing babes (twins this time). It goes by so fast, it's worth sacrificing to be a full-time mom!"

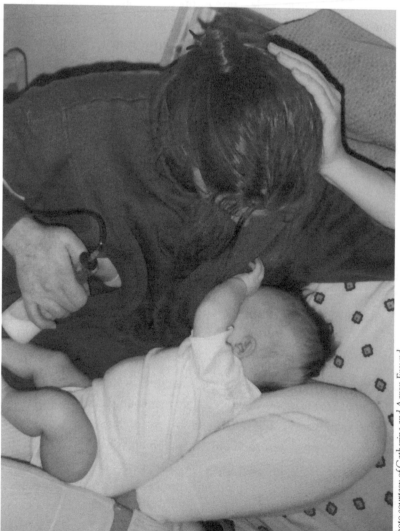

photo courtesy of Catherine and Aaron Freund

"I imagine my baby nursing; I also try to visualize the milk flowing out of my breast. Relaxation and comfortable, non-stressful surroundings help."

"I had problems pumping and finally gave up."

"I find it easiest to pump in the morning, when my breasts are full. I lie on the bed, nurse on one side and pump on the other. I get much more milk this way than pumping without baby!"

"A hand-held plastic pump works okay for me. I've never been very successful at expressing large amounts. I express while in a warm shower/bath."

"My friend had trouble getting milk to flow when she wanted to pump, so she used lots of pillows to prop her baby to her breast and would get him started on one side. Then her hands were free to use the pump, and her milk would flow well."

"You need to massage breasts and stimulate a letdown first."

"Best letdown is when I am watching the baby play or can hear her voice."

"I hand-express and donate to the milk bank. I never liked pumps. I have baby nurse on one side and pump the other. Milk flows real well."

"I didn't have much luck expressing. My daughter would never take a bottle anyway!"

"I used an electric pump for my preemie, but be careful: I started producing six ounces a feeding when the baby only needed two."

"Remind mothers pumping that it can take longer to pump the breast. I need thirty to forty minutes to get four to six ounces."

"I've tried several pumps (non-electric) and could never get as much milk as when I manually express it (I use a funnel)."

"I work outside the home and pump regularly. I have two electric pumps. I use one on each breast while pumping at work. This cuts my pumping time in half. Never could use a manual pump."

"I usually take a hot shower first and use warm compresses and bend well forward while sitting comfortably in a chair."

"The only way I can let down to pump milk is to have my baby start it by sucking, then quickly wash my breast and start pumping."

"While in the hospital with my oldest daughter, I had a need to express for my infant. I tried with an electric pump but found that manual expression worked best. (As it turned out, my husband ended up just bringing the baby to me every four hours.)"

"At first I pump in short strokes, similar to baby's sucking, to get things started. Once I let down, longer strokes are fine. Getting a good seal seems to be the crucial element for me. I use a little milk around the rim."

"I tried hand, cylinder, and battery-operated pumps. By hand worked best, but still not great. It helps to take fenugreek capsules and brewer's yeast, and I drink Mother's Milk Tea (by Traditional Medicine) with a tea ball of fenugreek seed added. I found the tea relaxed me and increased my milk supply."

"Pumps are like medieval torture machines!"

"I seem unable (or maybe too impatient) to pump my milk. I can't seem to do it!"

"For expressing or pumping, put feet up, breathe deeply, and apply a warm compress to breast before pumping."

"I work thirty hours a week and have given my baby breastmilk exclusively. He is five months old and it has worked very well pumping twice a day. (I am gone from him for ten hours.) I love my cooler and pump. I have found that in order to get milk to let down it helps to gently pull on both nipples or on one while beginning to pump the other. This simulates the baby's sucking and is *very* successful for me. I try to feed him more in the morning, evening, and during the night to make up for the time we are apart and to stimulate more milk production. I would also recommend starting to pump after or during a feeding in the first few weeks after birth to get used to pumping and to store milk ahead so you have "emergency" excess. Visualization and relaxation techniques are also very useful."

"Drink plenty of water, juices, etc."

"Expressing first thing in the morning or after a long period of separation often makes the milk come faster."

"Patience!"

"Relax, relax, relax!"

Obviously there is a wide range of experiences in everything from the amount of milk mothers are able to express to the techniques and pumps that have worked for them. Success with expressing milk depends, to some extent, on our bodies' individual differences.

The ability to relax enough to let down your milk varies from woman to woman and from time to time. There is tremendous variation in the size of nipples, and different breasts need stimulation in different places. Pumps with size adjustments for different-sized nipples are available, and electric pumps are quite popular. Directions for using your hands to "milk" your breast can be found in *The Womanly Art of Breastfeeding* and other books on the subject. ♥

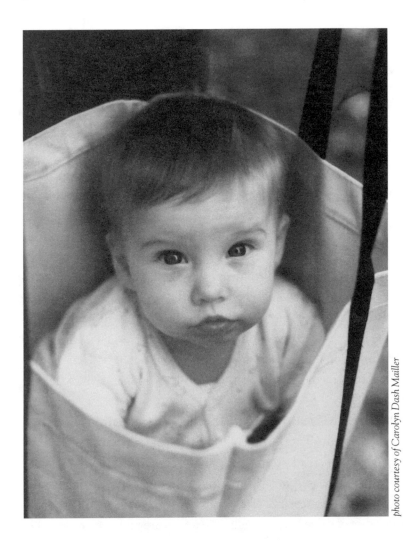

photo courtesy of Carolyn Dash Mailler

How Breastfeeding
Saves You Money

BY JODY WRIGHT

How much money does breastfeeding save you? The real cost of bottle feeding and the relative savings of breastfeeding are not easy to measure—but they do add up!

The most obvious savings to the breastfeeding mom is in the cost of formula. A one-quart can of pre-mixed formula costs about $3.25 here in Massachusetts (1996). Concentrated formulas and powders that require more work are $2.25 to

$2.75 per quart. Figuring a can of pre-mixed formula each day, six months of exclusive breastfeeding would save you $585 in formula costs alone.

Of course you need bottles, nipples, rings, and covers. If you want to have enough bottles on hand to wash them just once a day, you need 8-10 bottles. My calculations come to about $14 for this. As these tend to wear out and get misplaced, that cost might double. Sterilizers, bottle warmers, and other equipment are additional expenses. For disposable bottles, you could spend around $60 in six months. Refrigeration for opened milk, heat to warm bottles and sterilize water, and extra trips to the store when you run out of formula all add to bottle-feeding expenses.

The parents of a bottle-fed baby may also need to budget in supplementary vitamin drops, and may need to introduce solid foods earlier. A parent choosing prepared baby foods and cereals could find the price of 25 cents to 70 cents a jar adding up quickly at a time when breastfeeding mothers are sitting back in an armchair nursing and conversing with their babies. Viola Lennon of La Leche League International estimated a number of years ago that a six-month supply of formula and baby food equaled the price of a major appliance or of cleaning help for that length of time.

Of course, the breastfeeding mother needs to eat well and may choose to take vitamin supplements, but the actual increase of caloric needs is not substantial. It is the equivalent of an additional peanut butter sandwich and a glass of milk each day. Many pregnant and nursing mothers find this an ideal time to improve the quality of their diets: to eat more fresh fruits and vegetables, whole grains, beans, etc. The added cost of these may be negligible if they are replacing relatively expensive prepared and processed foods.

The breastfeeding mother will usually want to purchase special bras that give extra support and open easily for nursing. While the bottle-feeding mother may also need to purchase new bras during and after pregnancy, she may be able to find less expensive ones in a discount department store.

Postpartum clothing, too, will be an expense for both nursing and bottle-feeding mothers. Many separates in a basic wardrobe will work well for nursing. Clothing designed specifically for nursing mothers is often more expensive because it is made in small quantities and requires more fabric and stitching for the nursing openings. Some mothers purchase breast pumps ($15 to $125), lanolin, and other nursing aids.

More difficult to measure are the many ways you save money over a lifetime by nursing your baby. You may save substantially on doctor bills, hospital costs, and time home with a sick child. I once heard a long list of illnesses and problems that were experienced at much higher rates by people who were bottle fed as infants. The list included such things as heart disease, mental illness, headaches, and many more. For example, the risk of acute gastrointestinal illness in infants receiving formula was six times greater than in infants receiving breastmilk and 2.5 times greater than in infants receiving cows' milk (J.S. Koopman, MD et. al., Am. J. Public Health, 1985). Children who were formula fed or breastfed for six months or less were at increased risk for developing cancer before age fifteen.

Mothers of sixty-seven children were asked about the types and durations of illness requiring medical care between sixteen and thirty months of age. Breastfeeding was noted to decrease the number of infant illnesses and indirectly improve toddler health (E.E. Gulick, Pediatric Nursing, 1986).

Nursing your child exclusively for six months to a year can reduce his or her chance of developing allergies later in life. Breastfeeding, even for a short period, is clearly associated with a lower incidence of wheezing, prolonged colds, diarrhea, and vomiting. These differences are due to the antibodies in breastmilk that are provided to the baby as long as nursing continues.

The breastfeeding mother, too, may benefit from better health. Breastfeeding helps the postpartum body return to normal more quickly, and the risk of breast cancer decreases as the duration of lifetime lactation increases. Frequent and exclusive nursing postpones the return of menses, allowing greater recovery time between pregnancies.

With all the money you save nursing your baby, it might be more affordable to be a full-time mother or cut down on the hours you work, reducing child-care expenses. Since nursing provides the mother with a whole array of mothering hormones to help her feel more satisfied with her parenting experience, she may even choose to spend more time with her baby.

There is a good reason for everything in nature, and breastfeeding—with its documented benefits to baby, mother, family, and even the bank account—is no exception. ♥

Motherwear photo

The Art of Discreet Nursing

BY JODY WRIGHT

When I was in India several years ago, I was amazed at the Indian women's ability to wear a seven-yard piece of cloth with absolute grace. When I tried to do it myself, I had to rearrange and re-wrap every time I stepped out of a taxi.

Learning to nurse discreetly is also an art, but one we have few chances to learn. Like a woman in a sari, we can keep ourselves covered by adjusting our clothing as we nurse. Practice and the right choice of clothing can make it easy to nurse without others knowing. Here are some ideas for nursing inconspicuously in public.

First, choose a good place to nurse. You can nurse in your car before going into a store or restaurant. When dining out, choose a seat away from the traffic flow, and face away from people. Get to know the private places in your favorite mall or downtown area. Support restaurants and department stores that have lounges and changing areas, and ask others to provide them. If you can't find a place to nurse in a store or mall, tell the management. Maybe they've never thought about it!

When you are with a group of people, look for a place where you can turn away from the group to start nursing. You may want to find a quiet place at friends' homes to nurse. Taking a break and reconnecting with your baby keeps both of you happy longer.

Also important are clothes that are easy to nurse in. Many women have found that specially designed garments make it very easy to nurse discreetly in public. The trick to nursing discreetly, whether you are wearing nursing clothing or separates, is to have your breast and your baby's mouth meet just inside the nursing opening or an inch or so under the edge of your shirt hem. The fabric should rest lightly on your baby's cheek so she or he can still look up at your face. If you like more covering than that, you may want to drape a light blanket or scarf over your shoulder and your baby. Any way you choose to cover up, be sure there is plenty of air circulation near your baby's nose.

When you are nursing in a public place and you don't want people to notice, try to avoid watching your baby. Others will follow your gaze. Instead, look straight into people's eyes (they'll tend to smile and look away without even looking down), or continue to converse with your companion just as you would if you weren't nursing.

A situation that might test your skills is nursing in an airplane. I usually ask the flight attendant to re-seat me if I am next to someone who I suspect will feel uncomfortable with my nursing. A light flannel baby blanket will help keep a baby warm, even with the temperature fluctuations of a plane, and can be used to cover you both while nursing. Also keep a washcloth or diaper tucked in the seat pocket for accidents.

Another challenging situation is nursing at the beach or pool. A giant-size beach towel is great for a cover-up. (Be prepared for gusts of wind!) Bathing suits designed for nursing can really come in handy.

All of these tricks can be practiced in front of a mirror or with the help of your partner or friend. There is really no reason you should ever have to show your breast in public; with a little practice, you'll master the art of discreet nursing. ♥

photo courtesy of Tannis Longmore

Mothers Share: Our readers discuss
Nursing in Public

COMPILED BY JODY WRIGHT

This is clearly an issue that affects every nursing mother, and we appreciate the many replies we received. While some mothers don't feel comfortable nursing in public, there are many who have conquered the initial shyness and public disapproval. For others, it has never been an issue.

Many mothers feel overwhelmed by their complex roles as working women, companions, sexual partners, care-givers, and nurturers. Our society doesn't make it easy. As you read on, you'll see how breastfeeding moms have encountered everything from antagonism to acclaim.

Mothers Share asked: How do you deal with nursing in public?

"Just do it!"

"I am not shy about it! Why should my child cry and go hungry because of another's hang-up? She won't. Nursing is a natural thing. We can change others' attitudes by not hiding."

"I have come full circle. At first I was shy about nursing in public, and now I look for opportunities to do it. I believe a nursing mother makes a positive impact on everyone who sees her. And who knows what future mother may be influenced by seeing me!"

"I've had people come up to me as I nursed to remark on my pretty sleeping baby! I don't cover myself up with a blanket as I nurse. I believe that brings attention and makes people think I'm ashamed, which I'm not!"

"I nursed my five-month-old daughter on Main Street in Wall, South Dakota (tourist trap), and no one gave me a second look. We nursing mothers worry too much!"

"I hope that I'm not merely in a lucky minority when I say that no one has ever looked askance at us, not even at an elegant New York City gallery. (In fact, my baby was almost as much of a hit as the paintings and sculptures!)"

"I have always been fairly bold about public nursing, but I have had problems with the men in my own family (brother, father, father-in-law) feeling uncomfortable and making their feelings known. I also worry that I will feel more inhibited as my baby gets older—he is one year now—and fear I will face disapproval."

"I am still quite shy. My baby is a social nurser: likes to jump up every so often and see what's going on, thus leaving me exposed."

"I no longer nurse, because I did not have any support. Next time around I won't be shy about asking someone to come help take care of me."

"I'm usually out with my mother, who is very old-fashioned—she would die if I tried it. I go to the ladies' room and stand in a stall!"

"I personally do not feed in public, as I feel too uncomfortable. I feed him in the car."

"The only thing I was never able to cover up (and most of the time didn't want to) was Samantha's contented, yet noisy, eating habits. The happier she was the louder she 'purred,' hummed, and slurped. This, combined with her happily patting my chest or playing with her feet while nursing, made discretion difficult at times!"

"An easy-to-open and -close bra is a must!"

"At first, I practically hid under a tent of receiving blankets in order to be 'discreet.' I think you just have to get it in your mind that if someone is offended by breastfeeding, it is their problem. Just chalk it up to ignorance. What helped me most was a waitress who took the time to congratulate me for having the courage to nurse (it did take courage!)"

"At first, I was very shy and went through an elaborate ritual of arranging blankets over the baby's head, my shoulder, etc. My parents were still horrified that I'd dare do 'that' in public! (Once I was even asked to leave the room while at a friend of the family's house for dinner, despite the blankets!) Now I nurse openly in a light blanket when in a restaurant or store, etc. I've had few comments from strangers but lots of dirty looks."

"If people stare, I take comfort in the fact that my nursing helps them get used to seeing it, as more and more moms are breastfeeding—a fact of life!"

"The guys at work say it's very relaxing to see me nursing my son."

"Nursing tops make it easy to nurse in public!"

"For me personally, there's not much to deal with. I'm Muslim, and as such, I wear the 'hijab,' a long scarf covering. Whenever my babies have wanted to nurse, I've just covered them under the front of the light, soft fabric and off they went. I nurse anywhere and everywhere and nobody's ever bothered me about it."

"I feel a bit nervous now that he's older, but I figure they'd rather see a nursing toddler than hear a screaming one!"

"I didn't think I'd do it, but when my boy was hungry, his needs came first."

"I try to avoid people and places hostile to children with attached parents, and I respond to all comments with humor (good for letdown)." ♥

photo courtesy of Carol Ingber

When It's Time to Wean

BY BETH HERSH

There comes a time in every relationship when things begin to change. The way things were, the dear ways that were so satisfying, start to bring on a slight bit of irritation and restlessness.

So it is with our children. We hold our new beings so close and glory in their perfection. We pour our hearts and souls and all our physical stamina into creating just the right environment for these precious ones. We learn their needs and our own new ones. And we learn how to adjust, adapt, and give. And give. It becomes easier—the endless routine of diapers and burps, of hungry cries and satiated, milk-smeared, sleeping faces. It begins to fall into a rhythm so perfect that even with its endless variations, we still believe we have found the way.

Then a new idea grows within us, that the time will come when this child will no longer be nourished at our breasts. She will stand up on her feet, gather all her strength and determination, and take her first steps out into the world.

How do we know when the time is right? I remember holding my first little nursling and telling her that she could nurse just as long as she wanted. I meant it, at the time, with all my heart. She grew some, and I grew some, and somewhere in my second pregnancy, I weaned her. It was clearly the right time for us.

I believe the right time to wean is when one of the parties involved no longer wants to nurse. Sometimes it's the mother who wants to wear different clothes, get herself ready for a new baby, or just leave behind the demands of breastfeeding. Sometimes it's the child, ready to explore his world from a new perspective, who resists the retreat into that particular comfort. Either way, when someone's heart is no longer in it, it is time to begin the weaning process.

Weaning *is* a process, a process that can be so gradual that often it's difficult to know when it actually happens. Weaning begins when the first bit of nourishment goes into your baby's mouth from a source other than your breasts, and it ends when offering to nurse is no longer an option either of you consider.

Every nursing couple chooses the right time and the right way to begin. La Leche League recommends that you wean "gradually, and with love." This means, in effect, cutting back long before you plan to stop completely. Some people start by phasing out one nursing time each day. Others keep all the nursing sessions intact but work on the duration of each. Some mothers find that when they have eliminated a particularly troubling nursing time, maybe in public or in the middle of the night, things are easier and the plans for weaning can be shelved for a while.

When considering weaning your little one, it is important to understand what nursing means to her. Nursing brings her very close to you. She can feel your warmth wrapped around her while her tummy is being filled with sweet, warm milk. Nursing comforts her when something is wrong in her world. Hunger becomes a less important reason for nursing.

What worked well for me when I decided to wean my last child (we didn't have a pregnancy with its subsequent change or disappearance of milk to spur us on), was to put myself in her place and figure out exactly what she was getting from me. For her, the milk didn't seem to be the most vital element. She reveled in making eye-contact, being held, and playing little patting games. These became the things I would do for her when she asked to nurse. She enjoyed them, and they satisfied her most of the time. When they didn't, I would nurse her. Weaning is a process, after all.

For the times when only nursing would do—at bedtime or when she got hurt—I added a new dimension to nursing. I sang to her as she nursed, or I rubbed her back. I called this our "transition time." I did this every time so it became as familiar to her as the milk. Then I gradually shortened the nursing time and kept up the songs and rubs. I found it became easier for her to let go of the nursing, because she still had a lot of the precious associations. We were able to maintain close contact in a way that was special to her, and the actual nursing became less important for both of us.

I can't help but compare this method to those suggested by many parents and doctors: "The only way to wean a child is to abandon him, to withdraw from him either in his presence or by going away from him completely for a period of time." The first way involves keeping him so busy that he never gets a chance to ask to be close to you at all, let alone nurse. The second way is to go on a vacation without him and hope that when you return he will no longer ask to nurse.

I believe there is tremendous risk involved in either method. Our young children's self-esteem is so bound up in how we respond to them that any change feels threatening. When it involves a relationship so based on comfort and trust, we risk that they will never again trust us on the same deep level.

If you suddenly stop being there for them in a way they have come to depend on, their only choice is to believe that they did something wrong. The only way around this is to be honest with them. I believe that at any age a child can be told that someday they will not nurse anymore, but that you're going to look for something else you can do that is special. This might make them nurse frantically for a few days, but once they see that you are describing a process (one that can take them as long as they need) and not an event, they are usually able to let go little by little.

The letting go that's involved works both ways. It's easy to feel torn about weaning. It is a really big issue, and there is a lot at stake. It is a conscious decision to let the child grow in a new way, one that will take her farther from you than she has ever been. It's important to be prepared for grieving. No one told me this, and I was so surprised at my grief when it had been my decision to wean. There is always some sadness involved in loss no matter how wonderful the replacement condition is. My remedy has been to remain physically close to my little one, while at the same time reminding myself of my delight at each new growth step she masters.

Nursing is an intimate act that involves two very inter-connected beings. If we are able to treat it with the consideration it deserves, we should be able to glide through weaning smoothly and with all that is truly important still intact. ♥

photo courtesy of Pekka Hall

Parenting

We expect it to be easy, because everyone seems to manage it. But oh, how easy it is to feel inadequate! "Are we doing the right thing?" we ask ourselves. "Why is this child acting this way?"

Parenting is one of the hardest jobs in the world. There are no monetary rewards, no set hours, no certain milestones of success. The struggle to parent our children can bring out our worst and our best. It can cause us to come into conflict with our children, our spouses, our families, our friends, and our communities. It can bring up old pain from deep within us, but it also gives us joy, growth, insight and an experience of love and connection we'll get nowhere else.

Parenting forces us to grow and change almost every moment, it seems. We must come up with new solutions for the unique problems our children and circumstances present us with, because every family is made up of precious individuals with their own needs, perspectives, motivations, and moods. Being a parent is so much more than diapering and burping, feeding and clothing. Our children challenge our minds and hearts to adjust our points of view to theirs.

For each of us, the circumstances will differ, but there is one truism in every parent's life: We have a need to show love to our children and to receive love in return.

photo courtesy of Lee and Duane Hanson

Something Wonderful About Toddlers

BY BETH HERSH

As I watch my youngest sleep after a long, exasperating day, I realize I am fit for nothing but falling into my own bed and hoping tomorrow will be easier. It is not a restful period, this life with a toddler. It seems that even though I run at full steam all day long, I never really get anywhere. The laundry is still in piles on the floor, and I haven't turned on the computer in days.

No matter how much I seem to be getting done, my active little one always creates the need for more. Cooking is no longer a simple matter of making a meal; it often requires finding the pot wherever she might have taken it. Leaving the house means not just putting on a snowsuit; it usually involves a discussion about why we need coats and shoes, and sometimes ends with a screaming, kicking child being carried to the car.

And if the days are long, it seems the nights are even longer. My "big girl" doesn't seem to need me in her baby ways, but she needs reassurance that I am there for her in the dark of night. She often requires contact with some body part of mine in order to feel safe about falling back to sleep. Usually that means her foot in my face, and her foot in my face means I don't sleep at all.

Still, this is a magical time. She lives such a full life, I can't help but be charmed by the way she goes about her business of learning to grow.

Toddlers have the ability to live entirely in the moment. They are teachers to us in the way they are so alive and so true to themselves. While I might crowd my head with abstract ideas and philosophies of life and ways of getting through the day, my daughter is completely absorbed with delight in the progress of a marble rolling across the floor. And while I need to be aware of time and schedules, she needs to focus only on what is before her. She can give her full attention to how her zipper slides up and down without being remotely concerned with getting her coat on when I have an appointment across town in ten minutes.

You can try to teach toddlers rules, but on the whole they are un-civilizable. Rules are beyond their comprehension. The whole belief in rules rests on the belief that there is a future where consequences could happen and there is a past from which lessons might be learned. There is no past or future for a toddler. Her life is now, and anything that is not "now" is unthinkable.

That brings me to the events of each day. Parents of a toddler know it is risky to take them anywhere without toting a snack. When they decide they are hungry, there is no power on earth that will distract them. And mealtime? It is almost *impossible* to keep a toddler at the table for the duration of a meal. Most parents accept this and make as many kinds of portable food as possible. I have seen some amazing inventions baked into pie crusts and spread on bread so the toddler can eat a balanced meal on the move.

When hunger stops calling from the stomach, the other qualities of food are researched. Which foods are best for finger painting? Body painting? How many pieces can a cookie crumble into before there is no more cookie? Where does that cracker go when it's dipped too long in juice or milk? What foods roll? Which bounce? Which lend themselves to art, and which to science?

Toddlers are unable to lie. They can only report on reality as they see it. They are driven to tell it like it is—for them. Yet because their imaginations are so strong and their sense of reality as yet undeveloped, their version of truth may not always coincide with ours. A toddler can boldly tell you she didn't eat any pudding, though it's smeared all over her face. Because she knows she wasn't supposed to eat it, in her mind she never did.

Our toddlers love us passionately and completely. It is hard to find a purer love than this. When they are pleased with us there is nothing in the world they wouldn't do to show it. They love with their hands, their bodies, and their hearts. Every touch is a poem of love. My little one used to pat my face and gaze adoringly into my eyes. When a toddler throws his arms around your neck, you know you are loved.

Toddlerhood is a unique way of being. Even when they are displeased with us and our limitations, toddlers are delighted with themselves. And when they are displeased they let us know. To a toddler there is no concept of covering up feelings. We can read in their whole presence exactly where they are in any given moment.

I spend half my time running circles around my toddler and feeling as if I'm making no progress. She makes me tired, bedraggled, exhausted. But I allow myself to be grateful for her unique outlook and the lessons it teaches me about my own life. There is no question that I need her as much as she needs me, and I wouldn't trade this time for any other. ♥

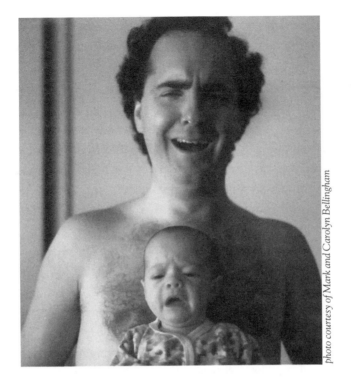

photo courtesy of Mark and Carolyn Bellingham

Helping Children Express Their Feelings

BY JODY WRIGHT

My friend Gay lives with four-year-old Claire, whose behavior is often challenging to those around her. One day as Claire broke into a tantrum, Gay tried reflecting Claire's feelings back to her. She invited Claire to do a drawing in order to express her feelings about her mother at that moment. Gay was delighted and surprised by how quickly Claire's anger subsided when she felt her feelings were heard and understood.

Feelings are our most personal possessions. If they are denied, we feel personally rejected. A friend spoke of his childhood this way: "My mother didn't ever allow me to have feelings. How could she love me? She didn't even *know* me!" Feelings don't go away when they're ordered to, but they do become less daunting when shared.

When I was child, I thought only children had feelings, that adults were somehow above them. Certainly my mother and father didn't feel the insecurity, confusion, love, and hate that I did. As I have grown, I've had to let go of this image that if I were truly mature I wouldn't feel insecure or emotional.

There seems to be a tendency in our culture for children to think that adults don't have feelings. We avoid letting children see us angry, we hide—or worse, bury—sadness, and we don't discuss our feelings with children in fear of destroying their image that we are strong, infallible adults. When we cover up our own feelings, we deprive children of the chance to know us, and we make it harder for them to express their own feelings.

One of the first steps in helping children express their feelings is to put our own feelings into words. You can start by expressing your daily joys and frustrations in ways that are not threatening to others. Expand your feeling-word repertoire (and your child's) by searching for words to express what you feel. When you find you are very upset by something, try using this formula: I feel _____ when you _____. Taking responsibility for your feelings rather than blaming others goes a long way toward building healthy relationships.

I've noticed that adults often act as if children don't have feelings. We lapse into ways of communicating with children that deny their feelings and humiliate or belittle them. We do this without intending to, because it's the way we were talked to (or at) as children. How can we stop this cycle?

Reflect back on childhood, and remember times you felt hurt or angry. Do you see your child having similar feelings? Watch for facial expressions to see what your child is feeling. One day as I began to yell at one of my daughters I saw her face drop, and my heart melted, along with my anger. I picked her up and hugged her instead. Since then I have tried to nurture that empathy. She needs love, not anger.

Children want to be heard. Active listening is a process of reflecting back to someone what you hear them expressing, then listening as they clarify your perceptions and give more information. Having someone listen to you is one of the most therapeutic ways to relieve feelings and often leads to the resolution of a problem. Next time your child hurts herself, reflect back her feelings to her: "That hurt! You really banged up your knee." You will be surprised at how quickly the tears stop when your child feels understood.

Even babies can be listened to. They say many things with their bodies and faces. By putting these communications into words for them, you are both listening and helping them learn how to express themselves. "You're feeling tired and want to sleep. Being around all these people has worn you out."

The universal language of communication involves touch, eye contact, and complete attention. Touch has the amazing ability to stimulate our hormones. When we touch one another, pleasurable and relaxing feelings often surge through our bodies, making us feel loved and cared for and safer about sharing ourselves. Eye contact and complete attention give us the trust we need to open up and risk being hurt in hopes of releasing feelings and being loved. Sharing feelings and being affectionate go hand in hand. ♥

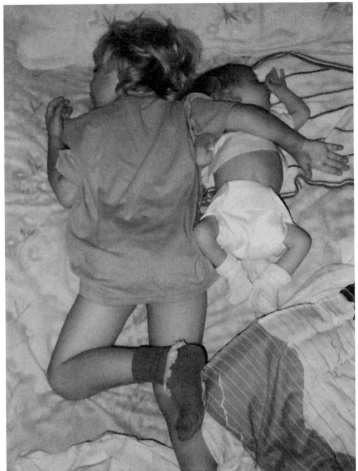

photo courtesy of Christine Lily

Becoming a Sibling

BY BETH HERSH

When I was thinking of how to tell Sara, my first born, that there would soon be another baby in the family, I knew it wouldn't seem like a very good idea to her. She was perfectly happy to have two adults whose worlds revolved around her. Anything I said would be akin to one spouse telling the other that he or she is so happy with marriage that s/he's going to bring home another partner to share the joy. Though I believed my daughter would come to appreciate her new sister or brother with a love that was unparalleled, this was going to be a hard idea to sell.

We began by giving her the facts: "There will soon be a baby in this family, and this baby will be our child and your sibling." We assured her that there was a special place our hearts that belonged only to her, and no one else would ever fill that place. We talked about how the baby would seem to take up a lot of time in our lives. He or she would need to be held, fed, walked, comforted, and cleaned almost constantly. But there would always be time for someone as important to us as she was, we assured her. This was something she needed to hear, and we told it to her many times both before and after her sister came.

Babies also need a lot of equipment. As time went by we took out all the baby things— seats, blankets, clothes, diapers—and let Sara explore their use with her dolls. She became particularly attached to a tiny outfit that was once hers, so we let her keep it.

It is important for kids in this situation to feel some control. They don't need to be calling all the shots, but they do need some real proof that their needs will be heard and responded to. I found that by giving in whenever I could, whenever it felt okay, it was easier for her to accept the times when I couldn't. I was able to give her that little stretchy suit, as much as I would have liked the new baby to wear it, but I couldn't give her the stroller. At two and a half she didn't have a clue about comparative value. All she knew was that I was respecting her need to hold onto something from her babyhood by not giving everything to the baby.

Children that age, or any age, really, have no idea what to expect of a new baby. Maybe they expect a fully formed child their own age. Many of us have no experience with newborns. Children need to be told as clearly as possible what a new baby is like. She won't play. She may not respond to them at all at first. New babies are not the babies you tend to see in the supermarkets or when visiting relatives. They are tiny, fragile, red, wrinkled, and somehow otherworldly.

No matter how well you ready your child (or yourself), there is no way to be completely prepared for a baby coming into your life. It is another experience entirely, and the arrival can't help but shock the whole family in some way.

I have seen new big siblings walk around in a state of disorientation for days after a baby comes. There is a tremendous amount for them to assimilate, and they usually have to process it alone. Small children don't know how to put their questions into words yet—they probably are unaware that they even have questions. They are trying to make sense of a cyclone while everyone around them is caught in the whirlwind.

There are many ways to remind your little one that he or she is still very special to you. The most valuable gift is your attention. Each day, tell her you love her in a thousand different ways. Praise her. Tell jokes and laugh at hers. Tell her stories of when she was a baby and the things she used to do. Remind her of the care you gave her, just as you're caring for the baby now.

Hold your older child close. Children have a fear of being forgotten and overlooked, and physical contact is most reassuring. Rub his arms, his back. Brush his hair and teeth. Cuddle and hug until he's ready to let go. Read or tell lap stories—what you're saying isn't as important as the fact that he's on your lap.

Let him come first sometimes. It's true that a baby needs immediate attention most of the time, but not always. Sometimes you might be in the middle of a cuddle or a book when the baby wakes up and cries. I used to call out, "I'm in the middle of a story with Sara. I'll be there in a minute." Then Sara knew that I placed a real value on my time with her. I really couldn't let a baby cry for too long, or too often; that's not the kind of mothering I wanted to teach her. But the act of calling out to the baby and asking her to wait made Sara beam with pride. Usually after a minute or two she'd say, "I think you should go to her now." She got a double bonus: I chose her first, and she was able to give, by allowing me to go to her sister.

Help your older child adapt by bringing your baby into the center of your home life. Demystify the new creature by feeding, changing, burping, and cuddling him on the living room couch. Make him a fact of life. Involve the older sibling as much as possible. Teach him to let the baby hold his finger in her fist. He will be amazed at how strong she is. Let her suck and be pacified on his (clean) fingers. He can also sing to her, talk to her, stroke her, wind up her musical toy. When she looks deeply into his eyes, the bond will grow beyond measure.

Your child can also take care of you in a special way. She can fetch supplies, answer the phone (or bring it to you), turn on music, tell you a cheering story, get you a drink of water, and maybe even make you a snack. There are many ways to let your older child know she is big enough to do "real work."

It is a difficult and tricky adjustment for a child when another baby arrives. Any energy you are able to put into making him feel important or to remind him he is still and will always remain special in your life will go a long way toward feeding his self-esteem. And the bond between another child and a new brother or sister will strengthen. This is the root, the very beginning of the sibling relationship, and there's no better way to start than to plant it deeply in the soil of love. ♥

photo courtesy of Tineke Dahl

Treating Children as Equals

BY JODY WRIGHT

The shades were drawn, so I couldn't see the man outside. I could hear him very clearly yelling at someone. Was it at a child or a dog? At what was he hurling his power-packed criticism?

As I listened to his abrasive words, I began to get an adult perspective of something I was aware of as a child. People talk differently to kids than to adults. As I became more aware of these adult-child interactions, I found a word to describe the discrimination I witnessed. I call it "adultism."

Adultism hasn't been widely explored. Except in *Parent Effectiveness Training* and a few other books on talking to children, I haven't found much to read on it. But there has been lots for me to watch. With three children, I often see adultism in the way I act and in the way others act toward them. Here are some examples.

•My friend is the director of a pre-school. As parents come to drop off children, their eyes seek out the teacher, they say "hello" to another adult, but almost always ignore the children passing within inches of them. This is a common way of treating children in our culture: virtually ignoring them.

•A child comes into a room and slams the door, and she is immediately reprimanded. Would we be that quick to reprimand an adult, or would we let it go a few times before saying something? Ordering, directing, and preaching seem to play a major role in the way adults in our culture treat children.

• If a child is doing something that disturbs us, we expect him to stop. We seem to think that adults are doing important things, and children are doing unimportant things; an adult's "work" has higher priority than a child's "play."

• We often ignore children's rights to their bodies by doing things we'd never do to adults. In India, my children fought a constant battle against the "cheek pinchers." In our culture, there are head pats, hugs, kisses, slaps on the back, and tickling. Most children like to be touched, but they need to be listened to at the same time.

In many ways, our culture has completely different ideas of what is expected of a child than of an adult. When we talk of kids being "disciplined," we mean that they do what others want them to do. When we talk of adults being disciplined, we mean they are following their inner motivation.

What causes adultism? We conceive of a child in our culture as knowing nothing and of adults as the teachers who write on this blank slate. We see ourselves as being responsible for what, when, and how a child learns. If we believe that knowledge, maturity, and size make us important, then it is easy to treat children as inferiors.

But what if we broadened our view? What if we saw children as miraculous seeds holding within them all the potential for growth into dynamic human beings? They are full of curiosity, energy, and the ability to communicate right from birth—with smiles, tears, cries, and cuddles. They are spiritual beings, perhaps closer to a knowledge of God than we are. From this point of view, we are nurturers rather than trainers. We become gardeners for living beings rather than molders of formless clay.

If we look at children as whole beings, we see they are very spiritual, often closely in touch with that essence of life that we have lost. They have wills and personalities. In a holistic view of children, only their minds and bodies are undeveloped. Will, emotion, and soul are all similar to ours. Recognizing this, we can be empathetic to them. We can feel that they are very much like us and treat them accordingly.

How can we overcome adultism?

First, make eye contact with children, and give them your complete attention. Recognize them when you meet them, and include them in your conversations with others. Open yourself up to recognizing the cues (eye contact, body language, etc.) that let you know they want to be involved.

Listen to the words you use with children. Are they different from those you would use in the same situation with adults? Are you negotiating solutions or giving orders? Are you changing your tone of voice, talking down to them?

Take a course or read a book on better communication skills. *Parent Effectiveness Training* is a good place to start. PET will help you learn to say things that treat others as equals. It encourages problem-solving skills to help all parties get their needs met.

Stop before you criticize, and ask yourself if it's really worth it. Can you address the source of the problem rather than criticizing the child? Perhaps fixing the noisy door would keep it from slamming. That's a lot more constructive than getting angry at your child every time she comes through it. Or teach a child a better way to do something instead of getting annoyed whenever she does it her way.

Try "quiet" techniques. If I see my child using a knife she isn't ready for, I simply hand her a safer one. She isn't insulted, my needs are met, and she knows exactly what I mean.

Don't embarrass your child by disciplining her in front of others. If you have something to convey, do it discreetly, preferably with the child in your arms. Make it a two-way discussion, not a verbal attack. You may have missed something, or your child might have a point to make, too.

Try changing the way you think of children, starting with your own. Appreciate the amazing growth they're going through and the strength and will it takes them to do it. Listen to them, and watch their body language and expressions. Give them lots of love. It will open up their hearts and yours, too.

This is really the goal: not only to act with less adultism, but to *think* with less. It is easy to slip back into relating to children the way you were related to as a child, but being able to act differently even half the time is worth a lot. ♥

A Fine Line:
Popular Culture and Our Children

BY ZIPORAH HILDEBRANDT

It's everywhere. Girls wear pink, boys don't. Boys have buzz-cuts, girls wear pretty stuff in their longer hair. Female Muppets and bears sport an apron, a bow, a flower, while males have only fur. In the Disney film *The Lion King*, the boy has a life, a quest. Mom stays home, has babies, and gets dinner. (Incredible how Disney, without a word, devalued the hunting ferocity of lionesses to be less than what male lions do—lie around looking noble.) The girl lion follows the boy, is rescued by the boy, runs for help, and looks seductive at appropriate moments.

This is our world. How can we raise happy children who will be strengthened by their gender instead of limited in their self-expression?

Letty Cottin Pogrebin, in *Growing Up Free*, recommends changing the pronouns when reading to kids. About 80% of modern children's books have male main characters, and 80% of the negative figures in fairy tales are female. Even it out, swap the "he's" and "she's"—for your sons, too. It's just as important—maybe more—for boys to grow up in a world where girls are positive figures. And when you see an animal of undetermined gender, give it the benefit of the doubt: call it "she." It may be a struggle for you at first, but it's well worth the effort.

The worst offenders? "Do not censor the classics or ban sexist books," Pogrebin advises. "Use them as examples of what's wrong, hurtful, and ridiculous."

Some people restrict their children's choices of toys, clothing, and the media, believing this is the way to encourage healthy attitudes. Pogrebin banned actual toy guns, though not invented toy guns, from her household. There is certainly value to this, but it isn't enough. The older children get, the less control parents have, and the more fascinated kids are with the world outside parental control. Children can easily feel left out and deprived of what excites their peers. They can grow up with resentment and a feeling that they don't belong with the group.

I believe talking with kids and striving to understand their perspective is

photo courtesy of Lisa Tarmey

essential, in conjunction with whatever other measures work for us. Talk about why you won't buy that toy, go to that movie, read that book. Be willing to compromise, be sensitive to your child's feelings and needs. Children are surprisingly capable of understanding. Even before they talk, they understand a great deal about feelings. Honor their feelings, and they will honor yours.

My experience has shown that when I say, "No, you can't have that," without an explanation, my daughter resents me, and feels wrong and unloved. Engaging in a dialog about why I won't buy it for her shows her she is important, listened-to. She may still want that toy, but she won't feel unloved for not getting it.

Guns and dolls seem to epitomize the polarization of boys and girls. It is amazing to see the attraction of these objects for very small children, even toddlers. Parents laugh and say it must be genetic, but cultural influences play a big part in what happens after that initial attraction.

The shape and feel of certain things seems to be compelling to children.

Sticks, spoons, Barbies, guns—they all extend the reach of a child in space. They fit well in the hand. When waved about, they give the arm a powerful feeling of directed energy. Is it genetic that girls stop waving their dolls around and start dressing them, instead? Is it genetic that boys begin to favor guns, swords, and baseball bats? Pogrebin asks, "Is this because he's a boy, or is it because he's seen guns everywhere defined as the accoutrements of male power and glory? We'll never know the answer until our culture tells its children that weapons are not symbols of strength but signs of weakness."

Bruno Bettelheim, in *A Good Enough Parent*, cautioned against forbidding guns. He spoke of children's need to feel powerful, to influence the world around them, to feel safe and capable of protecting themselves. It is a difficult issue. If a child senses a parent's discomfort with toy guns, that will be damaging as well.

But guns are no longer mere imitations of things seen at the movies. Guns are around us, on TV, in the news, hidden in closets and dresser drawers, displayed in racks, carried openly into the woods each fall, or carried secretly, anywhere, by violent, unpredictable strangers. Playing with toy guns will not make children into one of these human instruments of violence any more than playing with fire engines will turn a child into a firefighter. And forbidding guns will not prevent a child from becoming a murderer.

There are people who do really bad things. As adults, we know we can't kill them all, can't put them all in jail, can't even know who they are until after the tragic consequences. But children, if they are not to be overcome with despair, need a sense that there is power in the world that fights against evil. They need a sense that they can partake of that power.

It is up to us as parents to interpret this need for power. I have encouraged my daughter's liking for swords, and discouraged guns. At first, I told her the sort of things my parents told me: Don't aim guns at people, guns can kill. She still wanted a gun. Then, I approached the issue from a deeper, more personal level. Guns, I told her, mean sad things for me, my husband, and many of our friends. When we see guns, we think of war, of death, of cruelty. We fought against a war when we were younger, a terrible war in which many people's lives were changed horribly. Guns remind us of that war. She hasn't said she wanted a gun since I shared that.

Giving a girl a Barbie will not cause her to be obsessed with her weight, her clothes, her appearance. Forbidding Barbies will not ensure her a positive, healthy adolescence and adulthood, free of dieting and self-hatred. Barbies are just one tangible example of how our culture sees women, in a blizzard of the same messages from TV, movies, billboards, magazines, shop windows, book covers....Plastic, obsessed with clothes, hair, and weddings, Barbie is everything we love to hate. But honestly, how many of us reject all those obsessions for ourselves? Do you have smooth legs, change your mind about what to wear to an important occasion, get your hair done, or wear heels, lipstick, and eye shadow? If girls didn't see in Barbies some relevant truth about femininity, they wouldn't have the same attraction to them.

Barbie can be seen as flawed, and played with just as one plays with a broken toy: with knowledge of its inherent problems. "Are Barbies like real women?" I ask my daughter periodically. "How are they different?" Most obvious—and frustrating—is that they can't stand up. Their feet are warped. And Barbies aren't soft and warm like real people. They look an awful lot alike, too, whereas real people come in all shapes and colors and sizes. "Would it be good if everyone looked the same, the way Barbies do?" There are some very interesting subjects for discussion here.

My daughter's Barbies exercise a lot. They are champion swimmers and divers, take long treks across deserts and up mountains, climb ropes, rescue one another from dragons and evil-doers, and ride their horses. Of course, they can't do all this wearing silly clothes. They need practical, sturdy shorts, shirts, and boots. There was a time when all they did was get married, over and over, but it passed. It's actually been months since she's played with them.

For me, there is a fine line between making my daughter feel weird, isolated, and different, and letting her delve too deeply into popular culture. I talk with her about everything I have an issue with: TV, junk food, coffee, cigarettes, liquor, McDonald's, Barbies, guns, clothes, movies, games, books. I ask her what she thinks of these things. I counter her misconceptions. I explain how advertisers and greedy corporations lie in subtle ways to trick kids (and adults).

She understands. She has become adept at seeing through commercials for junky cereals. She still wants some of them—she loves the glitter and excitement of the animated ads. But she understands that they are lies, that just because something tastes good or looks good, it doesn't mean it *is* good.

Physicists say that every action has an equal and opposite reaction. Macrobiotics say every front has a back. I have to trust that my words and values have weight. My words speaking honest truth are all I have against the huge, glitzy world that doesn't care a nickel for my precious daughter's soul. ♥

photo courtesy of Gabrielle Shatan

Magic Moments

BY BETH HERSH

I am a working mother . . . a mother who works full time . . . a working woman who is a mother. No matter how I phrase it, it is clear to me that I am doing too much. Mothering is a full-time job and then some, and I work outside my home forty hours every week.

Sometimes I feel like a machine, grinding out meals and snacks, sweeping through the house trying to bring to it some semblance of order, organizing chores and friends' visits and holidays and birthdays and homework. Sometimes a whole day will pass, or two, or three, and I realize I have not sat down with any of my children for the nurturing and bonding time we all need.

I wonder: What impression do they have? How will they ever know, deep in their hearts, that they are the most precious blessings in my life? Will they carry into adulthood the image of a mother who was always too busy, too tired, too often not even there?

The other day I was in the car with Maya, having just picked her up from her friend's house. I was hurrying home and wasn't thinking of anything other than what

I could make for a quick meal. When Maya started telling me about the fight she'd had with her friend that day, I didn't even realize she was speaking.

Then she started to cry. I pulled over and held her. She told me about her fight, and she told me about the hard times she had had since school started. Then she cried about all the losses she had ever experienced. I cried with her over the pets and people who had left us, the homes we had moved from, and all the things we had ever loved that we didn't have anymore.

When we ran out of memories that released sadness, we sat close together and looked around. The sky was darkening behind the trees. The leaves glowed with all the fire of a summer's accumulated sunlight. A flock of geese flew overhead in their perfect V formation, noisily announcing yet another loss. We cried again, gave each other one more squeeze, and started home.

We had shared a Magic Moment, a time when time stops, the outside world slips away, and my children and I open up and connect on a deep and powerful level. It is a time when our souls touch and we remember how much we love one another and why we are together.

The rest of that day, Maya and I felt a special glow every time we looked at each other. We had been reminded of how important our bond is and how minor all the details of our lives really are; that the primary reason we are together is to express our love for each other.

These magic moments cannot be planned or forced. They just happen. But I have found that setting up the day to include times of quiet closeness makes it easier for the connection to happen. Sometimes when I'm tucking the children in at night, they will share something deep about themselves. If a child hovers while I am in the kitchen, I make the space for her to talk to me.

My children are not lost to me because I am doing too much right now. We can survive this period of never having enough time if we keep remembering what is most important. If I make it a priority to let my children know they are loved, they will take that love and use it to nurture their beings and to grow to their most magnificent selves. If I can allow these moments to happen, my children and I will carry the magic for the rest of our lives. ♥

The Tao of Motherhood

EXCERPTED FROM THE BOOK BY VIMALA MᶜCLURE

Parenting is a spiritual path that can bring you great pain and great joy and can have a tremendous positive impact on your personality and behavior. I believe our children, unknowingly and with innocent trickery, teach us the deeper knowledge of how to be true human beings.

Detachment

A wise mother gives birth but does not possess. She meets the child's needs yet requires no gratitude.

Observe how great masters raise up their dearest disciples. Observe how nature raises up the plants and animals.

Great teachers take no credit for their students' growth, yet they will go to any length to teach them what they need to know. Nature requires no praise, yet it provides for the needs of earth's inhabitants.

Mother is the reflective principle, the balancing agent for the child. Like a guru, she allows the child to make mistakes and loves the child without condition. Like nature, she allows consequences to unfold and balance to be restored when it is lost.

She intervenes only when the right use of power is required.

Return

Throw away gadgets. Discard expert opinions. Forget the toys to stimulate intelligence. Don't buy devices to simulate what is real.

Return to the real. Connect with your children heart-to-heart. Let them gaze at you, at trees and water and sky. Let them feel their pain. Feel it with them.

Touch them with your hands, your eyes and your heart. Let them bond with the living, breathing world. Let them feel their feelings, and teach them their names.

Return to the uncarved simplicity.

Values

If you hold to the Eternal in thought, word and action, your children will return again and again to you.

Your children may not understand the depth of your parenting until later. They may question your values and say you are "weird" or not like other kids' parents.

They may say your life is boring or strange. Never mind. The wise are not caught up in appearances.

The Way is at times boring in its simplicity. Hold to it. The superficial eventually repels.

That which is real attracts every good thing to it.

Experts

The ancient mothers knew. There was no need for books and experts.

Today we have lost much. We need to re-learn the Way.

Be cautious about what the experts tell you. What sounds complex and clever may have no roots. Wisdom has no cleverness in it. It is pure and simple, and when it is practiced the results are obvious.

The wise assist a child's being rather than his doing. ♥

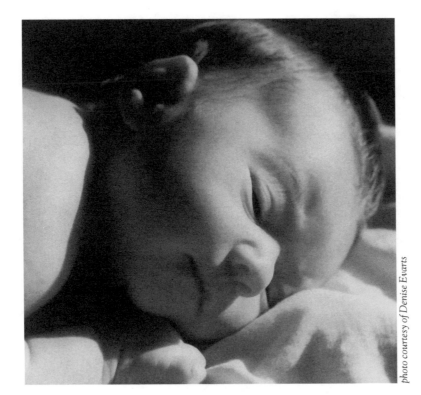

photo courtesy of Denise Evarts

Survival

They're supposed to be little angels "trailing clouds of glory"—and they are. Sometimes. Some of them. What about the others—the babies who cry and fuss and scream, keep us from the sleep we desperately need, demand more than we think we can ever give? What about moms who feel the bright dream of motherhood slide into the despairing shadow of postpartum depression? And what about those times everyone finds stressful: the first six weeks, the wee hours spent nursing, the holidays, and the emotional valleys? Sometimes all we can do is survive. In this chapter are words of support and wisdom—and some very practical advice—by moms who have been there. You'll find advice on how to stay a step ahead of the game, support for getting through another day, insight on what might be going on and how to get beyond the pain and frustration. We're all doing the best we can, but difficult times can seem as though they'll last forever. They won't.

photo courtesy of Lisa Tarmey

Getting Ready for the First Six Weeks

COMPILED BY JODY WRIGHT

You know, the birth wasn't so bad, but since then it has been so *hard*! I never imagined it was going to be like this. I don't get any sleep, my breasts are sore, the house is a disaster. I need help!"

This story, in each of its individual versions, is what I hear from many of the couples I work with. No matter what you do, the first weeks after you give birth are going to be some of the most challenging in your life; if you're prepared, they can also be some of the most rewarding. I asked a dozen moms what helped them get through those first six weeks. Here are some of their answers.

Prepare.

Stock up. Buy plenty of groceries, cleaning and laundry supplies, etc., and make sure that anyone helping you knows where everything is. You may want to put extra juices, bottled water, and hospital snacks on your list.

Organize your house well. You won't have a chance to do deep cleaning and organizing for a long time. Schedule the big jobs in your second trimester when you still have some energy. I put in new shelving to get organized and decided to invest in a dishwasher to help me deal with feeding three kids.

Moving? Consider carefully whether a move is really necessary. Many people move to a larger home during a pregnancy, but it can be really exhausting! It can also raise your cost of living, which you may regret when you find you don't want to return to work so soon. Babies don't need a lot of space of their own; they really prefer to be with you. Moving brings along its own challenges for a person under *normal* circumstances. It is particularly trying for a pregnant couple. Wait a year if you can.

Prepare food and freeze it, or get your friends to give you a casserole shower to fill your freezer. Plan some food for those last few weeks of pregnancy, too. I found myself emptying out my freezer to feed my family when I was exhausted in the third trimester.

Write some menu suggestions for your partner or for those helping you. Have all the ingredients on hand.

Make sure you eat well and take care of yourself during your pregnancy. Good health will make you feel better afterward, too.

Set up a place for you and the baby to spend time after the birth. I liked the pull-out couch in the living room because it got such nice sunshine. Set up your area with EVERYTHING you need to care for your baby: diapers, clothes, washing supplies, a squeeze bottle of water, tissues, baby blankets, changing pads, bottles of juice for yourself, good reading material, stationery, etc.

Arrange for some help.

Always plan for assistance after the birth, whether from friends, relatives, your partner, or a hired hand. You might think you and your partner can handle everything yourselves, but many couples find the experience overwhelming. Make sure your helpers understand that their job is to deal with the house, food, and laundry rather than the baby. The baby is for you and your partner. You will want people around you who respect your right to parent *your* way. You don't need someone judging you as you learn your new role.

Friends and relatives can be devoted helpers if you are clear about what you need done. How about having someone pick up the laundry every other day and bring it back washed and folded? Someone else can pick up groceries for you whenever they shop, then drop by and put them away for you. Other friends can bring meals or vacuum your house.

It is challenging to accept help. When someone offers, take them up on it. If you can't think of anything right then (new moms aren't known for their organizing skills), tell them you will call them back—and do! Tape a pad of paper by your phone to write down things you need. When someone calls and says, "What can I do to help?" tell them.

Remember: Your partner needs to adapt to a new role, too. It is great to have your partner involved in house and baby care, but don't forget partners also have to recover from the birth and get time to form a bond with your baby. When I came home from the hospital after my third child was born, the house was a disaster. My husband was exhausted and felt overwhelmed with responsibility for me, the two older children, the house, and a new baby. The days after the birth can be a real letdown for the coach. His big job is done, he's been up several nights, and he needs some caring, too.

Keep things simple.

Take care of yourself. Focus on yourself and your baby. Let someone else worry about the rest, or ignore it.

Don't clean house. There are times for clean houses and times for letting things go for more important pursuits. This is one of the latter, so don't feel guilty.

Consider using paper plates and cups. Use a diaper service, even if just for the first month. Have your partner drop clothes off at the cleaner's.

Arrange for friends to bring in meals, visit for ten minutes or less(!), and leave so you can eat in peace.

Be sure you eat regular, wholesome meals. This is one of the most important preventive measures you can take.

Continue to take prenatal vitamins, or switch over to ones designed especially for breastfeeding mothers.

Learn to nurse in bed so you don't have to get up at night. Install a night light or a very dim bulb where you can reach it easily, since at first you will have to see to "connect up" with your baby. This way you will get more rest and the baby will learn the difference between night and day.

Take it easy.

Plan to stay in bed most of the time for the first week postpartum. Mothers of two or more children often mention that they were active right away after their first birth, then regretted it when total exhaustion set in. "At first I felt so healthy, but it is amazing how soon I felt run-down!" At the next birth they resisted the urge to jump up and do things when that energy hit, and found they recovered much better as a result.

I started out allowing myself 15 minutes up every three hours and increased that a little every day. Sleep when the baby sleeps, even during the day. If you have older children, you will have to make arrangements for them so you can nap during the day. Perhaps you can train them to lie down or play quietly each afternoon. Though you will have to use some of your baby's sleep time to shower and eat, don't use it to launch a house-cleaning crusade, or you'll regret it later.

Limit your guests. Some mothers choose to observe the ancient "period of seclusion" after childbirth and decide in advance not to go out or have guests for a time. This allows them rest, special time for bonding, and time to build a new family. You may find that wearing a nightgown and seeing guests in the bedroom reminds them that you are still resting and they need to visit for only a short time. I have one friend who kept her robe hanging near the door. She put it on over her clothes when guests came so they would know she was still recovering.

Be very careful about how long guests stay. Let them know when you tire. One well-intentioned friend brought me dinner and stayed for an hour or so. Her visit was followed by an extended phone call. When I got off the phone, I was so exhausted I burst into tears.

Don't serve guests. They can get their own tea if they want some, and they can serve you.

Don't answer the telephone or the door when you are resting. The visitor will call again, but time for rest is very fleeting.

Prepare for nursing.

Read books and attend La Leche League meetings. Studies have shown that mothers who prepare for breastfeeding have fewer problems nursing and nurse their babies longer. Prepare before the baby comes by learning as much as you can about breastfeeding. Build a support system of people you can contact for help if you run into problems. It takes three to six weeks before nursing becomes smooth and easy. Hang in there; many problems will resolve themselves.

Throw out the clock. Particularly at night, watching the clock during nursing or feeding and noting how many times you are getting up will only increase your frustration. As one mom said: "Trust your baby, and trust yourself."

By the time I had my third child, I knew how hard those first weeks can be. I had an organized house, my mother to help, food in the freezer, some arrangements for the older two, and my husband home with two weeks paternity leave. I stayed home, mostly in bed, for several weeks. It was like a honeymoon for my baby and me. We lived in a rosy cloud with just each other. All the advance organizing was worth it for us, and it will be for you. ♥

photo courtesy of Rebecca Thiels

The Challenges of Parenting a Baby

BY JODY WRIGHT

Two years ago Prakash and I adopted Emily, our fourth child. We should have known what we were getting into; we had three older daughters, and not one of them was an easy baby. There were many times in Emily's first six months when we looked at each other and said, "Why did we do this to ourselves?" Parenting a baby is *hard work*! From months of sleep deprivation to the embarrassment of a tantrum in the middle of a mall, babies can be a real challenge.

Trying to maintain a day-to-day balance is a major part of the challenge. Your own health and mental peace are vital during these demanding months. Get help so you can take breaks. La Leche League, parents' centers, friends with children, and good books are all sources of help during the first few years.

I found changing my attitude to be the most effective (and sometimes the only!) way to "fix" a troubling situation. When my babies needed more of me than I felt I could give them, I'd get a good parenting book or a few back issues of *Mothering* magazine, some pillows, and some snacks, and I'd settle in for a day or a week of nursing and reading. By changing my expectations and settling in to fulfill my child's, the chemistry between us changed. My resistance had been causing over-dependence; when I stopped resisting, my children always seemed to relax their tight hold on me.

Emily is now two years old. She is happy to go off and be with friends. She loves to nurse and sleep snuggled between us at night. We no longer look at each other and wonder why we took on a fourth child. The joy she brings to our family says it all. ♥

Colic and Allergy: a Trying Time

BY ZIPORAH HILDEBRANDT

Six weeks after my daughter's birth, a childless friend came to visit. "How's it going?" she asked.

"She cries all the time; I can't put her down. At night, she wakes up every half hour and screams for twenty minutes. I massage her belly and she goes back to sleep, but she just wakes up again. We don't get to sleep until 3, sometimes 4 in the morning. It's horrible." I went on to describe my own depression and misery.

My friend responded off-handedly, "Well, at least she doesn't have colic."

"I think she does," I said.

It doesn't take a doctor to diagnose a colicky baby. But even with the label, what help is there? There are so many possible causes for colic—any severe, ongoing crying apparently from pain—and so few cures. As with so many circumstances of babyhood, it will pass in its time.

Fortunately, that was not the end of my friend's support. Her experience as an OB/GYN nurse prompted her to ask me about my diet—was I eating onions, garlic, spicy food? It was the first I'd ever heard about ordinary foods adversely affecting my baby.

Reluctant to give up any favorite foods, I made a chart. Each day, I wrote down what I ate at what time. I also kept track of the times my daughter nursed. I documented her crying spells, underlining once for severe, and twice for extreme. Within a few days, it was obvious that her worst crying came four to five hours after I ate onions, garlic, any kind of pepper, or any smoked food. When I cut out those foods, her worst crying spells diminished in intensity and frequency.

There is actually a long list of foods that can contribute to colic, but every baby is different. One study showed that most babies *prefer* a garlic-eating mom's milk.

Allergies run in my family; I have many myself. Antibodies are involved in most allergic reactions, and I knew that antibodies pass through breast milk—that's one of the reasons breastfeeding is so healthy. Why couldn't I be giving my daughter other antibodies as well, antibodies to food allergies? When I proposed this idea to my midwife, chiropractor, homeopath, allergist, and pediatrician, it was universally dismissed.

My daughter turned out to be allergic to dairy, wheat, soy, and peanuts, foods I was eating during those first months of nursing. Just last year (five years later), I picked up the revised edition of *Crying Baby, Sleepless Nights*, the most helpful book I'd found on colic at the time. There was an entire chapter called The Colic-Allergy Connection. I was vindicated, but too late.

My daughter's colic may have been caused entirely by a combination of my diet and her allergies. But there are many other possible causes, not least of which is the simple fact that an infant's digestive system is immature. This is why many colicky babies improve after three months, when their systems have developed.

Other possibilities include allergies to environmental factors, such as dust and perfumes; constipation; an ear, respiratory, or other painful infection; a structural problem, such as a dislocated hip; anal constriction or inflammation; a reaction to vaccination; and a number of other conditions requiring medical diagnosis. Some babies are temperamentally high-strung, sensitive and easily over-stimulated.

What can help?

•Carry your baby as much as you possibly can, in your arms, a carrier, or sling. Being next to you, moving with you, simulates the familiar sensations of the womb in a way that is very soothing, relaxing, and reassuring.

•Massage your baby. Touch is relaxing for both of you, and a massage can help tone digestion and move gas along more comfortably.

•Eat a variety of whole, unprocessed foods. Don't eat a lot of any one food. Sometimes a craving for a particular food, or eating the same food very frequently, can build up reaction/suppression that is similar to an addictive cycle. This can mask other symptoms of allergy.

•Chart your diet and the worst crying spells. Eliminate offending foods. Dairy foods, eggs, chocolate, caffeine, citrus, tomatoes, spices, onions, nuts, peanuts, beans, cabbage, and broccoli are common offenders.

•Try an elimination diet: don't eat any of the possible offenders for a week. If there is definite improvement, reintroduce one food each week in order to identify which cause your baby's reactions.

•Try going a week without deodorant, perfume, cologne, hair spray, or other scented products. Other family members and care providers will need to do the same. Use an unscented laundry detergent, and skip the fabric softener.

•Bear in mind that reactions to airborne allergens such as tobacco smoke, dust and mold, or perfumes and chemicals are quite common. Animal fur, lawn chemicals, cleaning products, carpeting, vinyl flooring, paint, detergent, hair spray, and

photo courtesy of the Smith-Bovés

countless other household chemicals can cause reactions by inhaling or skin contact. (Many are carcinogenic, besides.)

• Make sure your baby nurses fully from one breast before switching. An overdose of lactose-laden foremilk can cause gas and bloating.

• Don't be obsessed with burping. Most air swallowed during crying or feeding is naturally absorbed into the intestinal wall. The bloating apparent in many colic attacks comes from gas produced in the intestines because of too much lactose (milk sugar), an allergic reaction, or fermentation of cereals. Don't give any solids in the first six months.

• Consider trying homeopathy, which has provided relief for many babies (and parents). There are a number of helpful books available with information on where to get remedies.

• Last, but not least, don't blame yourself. Colic is not caused by birth order, your personality, or your parenting style. Chances are you're stressed and tense, but who wouldn't be in your situation? Get some extra support through this trying time. ♥

Dealing with Postpartum Blues

BY JUDY SNYDER

My feelings after the birth of my second child plummeted from exhilaration to utter despair. Months later, I learned I had suffered a postpartum depression.

The signs were there. "Why is it," I often asked myself, "that my friends seem much happier with their babies?" They were in control of their lives, while I was totally overwhelmed. I began my days with fears, uncertainty, and panic. I strained to make simple decisions, and cried for no apparent reason. Early morning awakening left me anxious and unable to fall back to sleep. I began to shut myself off from the people and activities I most enjoyed. "Am I going out of my mind?" I began to wonder.

My daughter was eight months old when I finally sought the help of a family therapist. Time and therapy anchored me once more. Other women have found help in homeopathy and in anti-depressive medication.

How does a mother know the difference between the typical "baby blues" and a depression in need of professional attention? The main difference is duration. Symptoms associated with typical blues fluctuate and persist just a few days. Feelings associated with postpartum depression (PPD) are more constant and can last for weeks or months.

Women may experience PPD immediately after birth or at any time during the next three years. It can follow the birth of a first child or a sibling, or it can occur after an adoption. A biochemical imbalance seems to be the most common cause of the illness, but other situational factors (a move, employment change, loss of a family member, etc.) can also contribute.

Approximately half of new mothers experience some form of depression, ranging from milder baby blues to more severe depressive states. Psychosis, with symptoms including delusions and thoughts of suicide or infanticide, affects one to four of every thousand new mothers.

Getting Help

PPD can be devastating to one's health and family. Early diagnosis and treatment are essential. An exceptional resource is *The New Mother Syndrome*, by Carol Dix, a book that describes the various states and stages of PPD and its treatment.

Depression After Delivery is a national self-help support group for mothers experiencing postpartum illness. Volunteers staff telephones across the country to help mothers going through an illness they once experienced themselves. Call (215) 295-3994 to locate a group near you. ♥

photo courtesy of Elisabeth Liebow

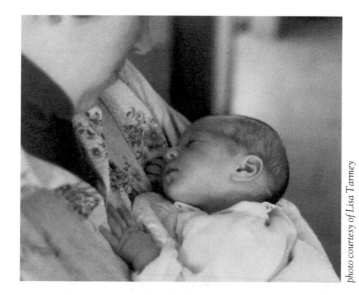

photo courtesy of Lisa Tarmey

Surviving Postpartum Depression

We asked two mothers who had experienced postpartum depression to share their experience. Here are their stories.

My son is now one, and I am almost over a year of depression. For the first four months I didn't recognize that I was "depressed." I didn't realize I was angry and sad about the surgical delivery of my son. I still find it difficult to refer to his emergence into the world as a "birth."

I wanted a home birth attended by my husband and a midwife. When labor began, I felt mentally and physically ready to give birth, but my body did not cooperate. After twelve hours, I had a premonition that my baby was not going to come out the way it was supposed to. In my heart, I knew I was doomed. The contractions became excruciating. After two days, I gave up.

My biggest fear was a hospital birth or a cesarean. I never confronted this fear while I was pregnant, but I sure had to now. We transferred to the hospital, where the onslaught of medical interventions began. I tried to disassociate from my body; I couldn't bear being there. I felt dead and have basically stayed dead since. Just writing this letter makes me so sad, it is soaked with tears.

My son was, and still is, perfect. When we finally came home, I was sick for several weeks. My little boy wanted to nurse every one to two hours, and all I wanted was sleep. I was exhausted and defeated. Except for my loving and supportive husband, I received very little support from family.

When my son was seven weeks old, I developed bronchitis, then asthma for the first time in my life. I sought treatment and went on the merry-go-round of antibiotics and yeast infections. I told the doctor who treated my asthma that I was depressed and he just laughed it off, saying it was normal. I was definitely not "normal."

By about month five, I didn't want to live anymore, yet people expected a bright, cheery New Mom, carrying on as usual. "Isn't being a mom just great? Isn't it rewarding?" I could barely talk to people at all, but when I had no choice, "Yes," would come the expected reply. I couldn't answer the phone and would turn it off. I never answered the door or went anywhere. I barely had the energy to wash and dress myself and my son. My husband cooked and cleaned and did the laundry and all the shopping. I cried several times a day and felt miserable. At night I felt like I was suffocating as my asthma was worse then, and I slept very little.

This mental and physical dis-ease was so unlike me. I had always been one of those healthy, "up" people who sees the positive in everything. Now I saw nothing positive in my life. I rationalized my situation. I was lucky and blessed to have a perfect baby who was breastfed and healthy, to have a wonderful loving husband, to have a home, car, and clothes for myself, and to have a career I could return to at any time. I tried to reach out for help. I called my midwife, who said I had to work it out and heal myself. She suggested contacting the Cesarean Prevention Movement, but I couldn't face their meetings. I looked for therapists who dealt with birth issues and found none. I knew drugs were not the answer and would only mask the problem. I continued to see my chiropractor, and found that spinal adjustments helped my asthma immensely.

Whenever I felt physically better, my attitude would improve. When my breathing difficulties were almost 100 percent improved, I began having some happy days interspersed with the sad days. I cried less, felt like killing myself less. I began to feel hopeful. I attribute my recovery to my willingness to seek and accept help, the support and love of my husband, and the expertise of my chiropractor and my homeopathic physician.

Homeopathy is what finally made the transition for me from self-hatred and death wishes to a confident, happy person. The remedy given me was what my body needed to step beyond this prolonged guilt and anger. Almost immediately upon taking it, I started to laugh, something I hadn't done in over a year.

Now I can answer "Isn't it great to be a mom?" with a resounding "Yes!" It is rewarding and fun. I feel I can explore the birth of my son and answer some of my questions. I can confront my feelings and resolve the dissonance, though that will take some time. We would like to have more children but I first need to heal completely, and I'm working on it.

My daughter is four now, and I have fully recovered from the depression that burdened me after her birth. With its attendant causes and effects of illness, anger, guilt, and dark memories, it has called into question almost everything about my life. It was caused by a mountain of factors, heaped upon my exhausted mind and body. No one thing cured it; it was a process as complex as living itself. The healing was in getting a handle on one factor at a time, gradually building back my strength, nerves, and immune system. I see now the positive outcomes of this bleakest period. At the time, though, I felt rage, grief, betrayal, and hopelessness.

I hated where we were living. I had no car or nearby friends or family, and I felt completely dependent on my husband, who worked into the evenings six days a week. I felt (mostly) confident about my baby's care, yet, oh, what a gap between my expectations and reality! My daughter was colicky and cried—screamed— almost all the time she wasn't asleep or nursing. I was ill, both from complications of the birth and from allergies that hadn't bothered me during pregnancy but returned in triple strength immediately after. Worst of all, the pain of my reactions was so beyond anything I'd experienced before that my homeopath, chiropractor, obstetrician, and midwife doubted it was caused by allergy.

Moments from the horrible first six months stand out vividly. I cried, unable to stop and unable to identify why, as I changed diapers, prepared basic meals with one hand, and did the laundry. I carried my daughter constantly so she wouldn't scream, and because of back and neck problems, a carrier was out of the question. Her screams were piercing, and made me feel that I would go over the edge of sanity.

I doubled over in pain as I hobbled in circles for hours, bouncing my daughter to keep her quiet. What bitterness I felt seeing the woman across the street out on the lawn in the sun, reading magazines while her baby slept in a carriage.

It got better in stages. Eliminating certain foods from my diet helped my daughter's worst screaming bouts. Moving at six months helped my allergies. A therapist interested in birth issues gave me needed perspective that yes, I was having an unusually hard time, and it wasn't my fault. Having new allergy tests and gaining understanding and control over complex physical factors were enormously helpful in recovering.

So many people turn away when a new mother speaks of pain or depression. But it's real, and it isn't anyone's fault. I was in mourning for the cooing, gurgling baby I didn't have, for the joyous, singing mother I couldn't be, for everything I had fantasized and dreamed of for years that didn't materialize. What *do* I have? I have a wonderful daughter and gratitude that a miserable time is over. I survived, learned, and grew from that suffering. ♥

How to Survive a Fussy Baby

BY BETH HERSH

It is six o'clock in the evening. You have just managed to prepare some semblance of a meal for your family and are about to sit down in the first chair to welcome you all day. Your family is assembled at the table, and steaming food reminds you that you haven't had a real meal in a long time. Just as you settle, with a sigh of relief, your fussy baby begins a wail that you know from experience is likely to last for hours. You get up, lift her from the cradle, and begin an evening of pacing, bouncing, walking endless circles around your house, and crying tears of anger, frustration, and sheer exhaustion.

There is little that can be more debilitating than a baby who cannot settle. That this comes at a time when you have to physically, mentally, and emotionally recover from the trauma of giving birth can wreak complete havoc on your health and well-being.

There are many reasons why a baby fusses and few, if any, that you are likely to have caused. This is the most vital piece of information I can give to the frantic parent. This is what would have helped me immeasurably to have known eight years ago.

From a world of constant motion and gentle sounds, steady warmth and ever-present food, your baby was expelled into a world where she has to deal with hunger, cold, loneliness, and fear. In that former world, all needs were met. Now she has to express herself to be taken care of. The language she is given to use—her powerfully moving cry—alerts you that she has a need and compels you to satisfy it. What it cannot tell you is exactly what that need is.

Most babies cope amazingly well with the adjustment to our world. In the arms of their loving parents, they discover nurturing and grow to trust. For some babies, though, no amount of loving care seems to help. Their immature systems can't handle what is required of them here. Their stimulus barriers are not developed enough to block out disturbing sensations. Their immature digestive systems are not

photo courtesy of Lynn Buhlig

digesting their food sufficiently.

With some babies, the startle reflex is very strong and they fear being handled or unsupported. Some thinner babies seem to have nerves very close to the surface of their skin, and they feel the cold or a scratchy fabric much more acutely than we imagine. For these babies, demanding behavior ensures survival, both physical and emotional. Fussiness alerts parents to the fact that their needs are greater than other babies', and they are cared for accordingly.

There are very effective methods of bringing relief to your baby. You do not have to put your life on hold and wait until he or she "outgrows" it. Try to duplicate the environment your baby remembers. In the womb he floated freely, every part of his body gently supported and softly massaged. The temperature never varied, hunger was unknown, fear and anxiety were quickly relieved, and perhaps most important, motion was constant.

All babies share the need for rhythmic motion. It centers in their vestibular system, in a tiny organ of balance located behind each ear. Here there are sensors for three directions of movement: side-to-side, up-and-down, and back-and-forth. The unborn child's vestibular system is highly sensitive and well stimulated. There is constant movement in the range of all three sensors. When a baby emerges from that environment, he has a very strong need for motion.

To give our "high need" infants the motion they crave, we have to cover the range of the three directions of movement in a gently rhythmic way. One way is what I call the "new-baby dance." With baby in your arms, sway side-to-side and jiggle her up and down gently. At the same time, walk slowly, dipping your knees a bit with each step, to give her the back-and-forth motion. It sounds tricky, but with practice it becomes habitual. My husband and I used to joke at social gatherings, because we could always spot people who had babies at home: they held their tea cups and swayed unconsciously as they spoke.

Another way to satisfy the need for constant motion is to invest in a baby carrier, if you don't already have one. When your baby is connected to you, your movements throughout the day will provide great relief.

Babies with immature digestive systems need a little something extra. Warmth and gentle pressure on a sore, gas-filled abdomen help a lot. Lay him across your arm with his cheek in the crook of your elbow and his belly against your flat palm (one variation of the "football hold"). As you bounce him gently, his weight puts pressure on his belly, pushing gas out. The other hand can massage the small of his back, relaxing him and helping the gas escape.

Infant massage is an excellent way to relieve your baby. In a very warm room with soft lights and soothing music (or better yet, with your voice singing lullabies or chanting in rhythm), your naked baby will melt into the loving touch of your warm, lightly oiled hands. A good stroke for pushing gas out is a circular motion clockwise below the belly button. Follow this by bending her knees gently into her belly and holding for ten seconds. Repeat this three times with firm yet gentle pressure.

The days of a fussy baby do pass. Still, I do not find the common advice of "waiting it out" very helpful. My firstborn was a thin, high-strung infant who had extreme reactions to cold, movement, and noise. I had believed that holding her a lot and nursing her on demand would keep her happy. I was shocked at the intensity of her distress even though I was doing more for her than I had believed humanly possible. My fragile parenting self-esteem was hit such a hard blow that when I heard friends tell of their babies smiling and cooing in their infant seats, I believed they were lying! Mine screamed and cried whenever she wasn't being nursed or walked.

I know what changes an uncomfortable baby can bring to your life. Recognize that this is a time of extreme challenge, one of the greatest challenges you will ever face. Let go of anything in your life that can be let go of, and gather as much support as you can. Now is the time to politely refuse the company of those who continue to give you "advice" that goes against what you believe in your heart. If the creative solutions you have devised (the nightly auto tour of your town, the 3 A.M. paces, etc.) work for you, that is all anyone needs to know. Now is the time to gather close those who would nurture you and care for you as you are putting out so much nurturing energy to your needy little one.

The payoff is immeasurable. For all the miles I paced with my daughter, the gallons of milk she consumed (and spit back) at my breast, the rude comments about "spoiling" I endured, and the sleep I didn't get, we emerged as a tightly bonded, loving unit. I am now confident of my mothering skills, sure of myself in other challenges, and more creative in working out solutions to any crisis. My daughter is a secure, happy, relaxed, and loving child. People comment on the ease and comfort with which she adapts to new situations.

I do carry regrets from that time: the moments I could not bring myself to respond once more, the times I screamed along with her (and hoped that my windows were closed and my neighbors were away). Still, looking back, I know I gave and gave and opened my heart and learned to give some more. She took and took and grew in faith that she would be well cared for and that there was nothing to fear. Sara's daddy and I did it our way—her way—and we know we gave her a powerful beginning that she can draw on for the rest of her life. ♥

Don't Sweat It:
Tips for Summer Sanity

BY ANDREA COLLINS

Are you wondering how you'll make it through the summer heat with children? Fear not! Here are some hints for a fun and comfortable season.

Things to Do

• If you're a new mom, try joining a "mommy and me" play group. They are usually held at neighborhood centers, churches, or hospitals. There are also mother/child exercise classes at many gyms and athletic clubs.

• If you use cloth diapers, avoid rubber pants or wraps. Skip a cover or use a breathable cloth wrap like Nikky's cotton or wool covers.

• Are your kids a little older? Let them take a cool shower fully clothed. They'll giggle and squirm and run outside soaking wet. Within minutes, they'll be dry and in much better spirits.

• If you don't care for water guns, try old (well-rinsed) spray bottles. It's better than throwing them away, and they're far less menacing than toy pistols.

• Plan indoor activities during the hottest hours of the day. Try reading, arts and crafts, the library, folding laundry (a family activity in my house), and board games. Taking it easy in the heat is especially important, as children can easily become overheated.

• Plan a trip to a museum or planetarium. These are great destinations when everyone wants to get out. The movies can also be a lot of fun, and matinees are inexpensive (especially if you sneak in your own popcorn).

• Join the Y or a local swim club. They generally have reasonable membership dues and offer other activities for children.

• If it's too darn hot, put up a tent in the shade. A tent can be a wonderful place to cool off, daydream, or read. It can be a "cave" or a "hideaway" for all ages to enjoy.

• Use this time to do your food shopping in an air-conditioned grocery store.

Everyone will feel refreshed, which might make the shopping-with-kids experience better than usual.

• if you are overweight, as I am, just the thought of summer can make you sweat. Try wearing men's boxer shorts under cool skirts. They keep your thighs from chafing and are cool and comfortable.

Things to Eat and Drink

• Try freezing fresh veggies. Teething babies and toddlers enjoy ice-cold carrot and celery sticks. My five-year old will eat broccoli trees right out of the freezer.

• Try keeping an ice chest, with a few containers full of juice, on your patio or in your backyard. Your kids can help themselves without having to come in and out.

• In the summer, my great-grandmother did all her cooking between 5 and 6 A.M. It's usually the coolest time of day as well as the most peaceful. Meals can be reheated quickly or eaten cold.

• Do you dread the all-too-familiar peal of the ice cream truck? To save money and have fun, make your own frosty dessert. It's not as difficult as it sounds. Blend a cup of frozen fruit (berries and bananas work best) and a quarter cup of lowfat yogurt in a food processor or blender for a few minutes. It's delicious and low in calories, and your kids will be amazed. ♥

photo courtesy of Katrina Hill

Taking It Out on the Kids

BY BETH HERSH

It is so easy to lose control with our children. They know all the buttons that push us to the edge, and they test them again and again. It is part of the process of growing that they have to keep stretching their limits and wielding every bit of power they can muster.

To those of us who grew up in abusive families, the issue can be quite serious; it can be one of our children's safety. Those of us whose families were not especially violent still need to manage anger wisely.

As natural as joy and sadness, anger can protect us by letting us know when people are pushing too hard or asking too much of us. What can we do when our children push us to the limit?

The most important thing is to separate yourself from the situation as quickly and completely as possible. Get to a place that ensures safety for you *and* your child, even if it means just leaving the room. If your child is not inclined to follow, that may be all you need. If that's not enough, close—even lock—a door. I have left my child alone, knowing that in her moment of losing control she probably needed me very much. Realistically, though, I couldn't be there for her. I knew if I had time to calm down, I could return ready to offer my love.

I will never forget one of those times. I sat on my front steps, head in hands, with the sounds of crying children audible through the door. A neighbor walked by, and I wondered what she must think of me. She, a mother of four, sized up the situation in an instant and called out, "Hang in there." Then she jokingly invited me to leave my mess, jump in her car, and go bowling. I felt so supported and understood, I was able to go right back in and comfort my children.

When you go to your safe place, it can help to do something calming. I drink a glass of water. Some people wash their face and hands. Try counting, singing a song, or doing jumping jacks. When you're over your anger, discuss what happened with your children; they understand a lot more than you might expect. Unless you raise the issue of your anger and how you're dealing with it, they will probably never talk with you about it. Opening the subject up for discussion allows them to release their fears and concerns.

There are other ways to relieve the pressure. Parental crisis hot lines urge parents under extreme stress to call a trusted friend, a family member, a counselor, or a religious advisor. Look in the phone book under Social and Human Services, Child Abuse Prevention, or Parent's Anonymous, and keep a number handy. A call can do wonders to defuse a tense situation or just to have a sympathetic ear.

What causes anger?

Anger most often arises from overwhelming stress, even if the stressor itself is not present. It may be triggered when you are late (*your* stress) and the children refuse to hurry, or when company is coming (again, *your* stress) and the children haven't cleaned their rooms. When anger escalates into a raging fury, it is a clear sign that you need to get some distance. Take time to calm down, and when equilibrium is restored, analyze the incident. Take it apart step by step, and see exactly what caused you to lose control. Once you become aware of the warning signs you can learn to separate yourself from a potentially volatile situation before it becomes a scene.

What causes you stress?

For me, stress often comes when I need to leave the house on schedule and I have to get my children ready to go. I have learned to get all the bags packed and to the door in advance. When I don't feel frantic at the last minute, I'm less likely to lose my temper.

Sometimes stress stems from our own neediness. If you feel that you're giving and giving when what you really need is someone to give to *you*, plan a treat for yourself. Find time to read or take a warm bath, or just give yourself a big hug. Take time to think clearly and start over.

Identify the cause of your anger.

Learn to identify the source of your stress and the cause of your anger. Anger that comes from buried stress tends to come out in surges of volatility that catch others off guard. When this happens, separate from your children as fast as you can. Put the baby in the crib, turn on the television, put out a snack if you can, and get away to your safe place.

When you calm down, explain and apologize to your children. How reassuring it is for them to hear you say that something else upset you and you didn't mean to be so hard on them. The details are not essential. The honesty is. By telling them you are sorry you lost control, you are also telling them it is not okay for them to be treated like that. This sets them up to value themselves and, as they go out in the world, not to accept abusive treatment from anyone.

If your anger, on the other hand, is clearly related to something the children have done, the strategy can be very different. You need to put into effect whatever plan of discipline you and your parenting partner have decided on. It may be a "time out," or discussing the matter with the children and coming up with a solution. You might need to separate them from each other so they can calm down. Teaching children about creating a safe place to go with their strong feelings is a tool they will use for the rest of their lives.

Whatever the circumstances, whatever the behavior, I do not believe it is permissible to hit children. Spanking teaches them that violence is okay if you are bigger and stronger. It robs them of self-esteem and the ability to work things out in a peaceful, respectful way. If hitting is a way of discipline for you, I urge you to read some of the excellent books on constructive, alternative methods.

Children's hearts are open wide. There is no limit to their capacity to forgive. Every story I've ever heard in which a parent apologized to a child for behaving inappropriately ended in the child beaming back love and acceptance and then running off to play, free and happy. What we must be careful of is that we don't ask them to take care of us. We apologize to them so they will know right behavior from wrong. What they offer spontaneously is what comes from their hearts, and usually it is just those things—love, understanding, and hugs. But to ask for them is to put the child in the role of caregiver, and that is not a fair burden for a child to take on.

That there is violence in this word is a fact we are forced to recognize daily. Whether or not there is violence in our homes is something we have a choice about. We decide what methods we will use to discipline our children and we, as adults, must learn to deal with our own out-of-control feelings. If we can do all this in a way that demonstrates respect and value for our children as well as for ourselves, then we will have solved one of the most difficult problems of child-rearing. We will be healing our children and healing ourselves as well. From there we will be actively healing the planet and contributing, in a powerful way, to world peace. ♥

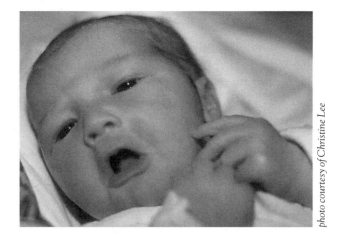

photo courtesy of Christine Lee

Mothers Share: Our readers discuss
Handling Criticism

COMPILED BY JODY WRIGHT

Our Western society is just emerging from a Victorian era of childrearing. In the last century or so, parents have been admonished not to touch their children except to perform the important physical functions. Even in the 1940s parents were told not to kiss their babies, to keep them on a strict schedule, and to let them cry. (Come to think of it, some "experts" still recommend that!)

As we emerge from several generations of almost exclusively bottle-fed children, our culture has lost sight of natural feeding practices. Current economic and cultural pressures on mothers to be employed have their own repercussions on parenting styles.

With all these factors, it is no surprise that there are many different ideas about how to raise children. As parents, we need to educate ourselves and explore the many options available. Ultimately, we are the only ones who can make choices for our family, and the choices still must come from our hearts.

Mothers Share asked: "How do you handle well-meaning criticism on how to raise your kids?"

"I have learned to be open to advice—once in a while it is very worthwhile. If it is not what I believe, I listen (important), and thank them (very important). Then if the situation calls for it I explain what I feel and believe, without picking a 'good' or 'bad' way."

"The least said, with a warm but firm tone and smile. 'We have decided on a lifestyle and way of parenting we feel good about.' Change subject. Be firm."

"I've come across a lot of criticism from my family, and not much of it is truly well-meaning. I try to let it all run off me like beads of water on a newly waxed car."

"Often times well-meaning critics feel better just saying what they feel, and so I listen and do what I think is best. When they say something that is helpful, though, I change my ways."

"I usually sit quietly and listen to them for a minute, then simply explain 'I do things because I feel they are right.' No one can argue with how you think or feel."

"If their suggestion sounds good, I first check with my doctor and/or nurse, and discuss it with my husband. If all four of us feel it could or should be tried, we try it. It may seem like a long process, but this is my first baby and I'm not willing to take any chances."

"The best support I have found for handling criticism is to read publications such as *Parenting from the Heart* and pro-breastfeeding magazines. From these sources and LLL meetings, I find my only encouragement for nurturing and nursing my baby."

"WAIT. In a year or two your critics will bear a child exactly like yours. For critics past the age of begetting babies, they are also past the age of remembering their children's childhoods. Use this understanding to increase your patience with people of differing beliefs."

"I'm learning that to disagree and argue isn't worth the effort. Every mother seems to be 'right' in nurturing her own child in her own special way."

"I don't handle advice or well-meaning criticism well at all. I get frustrated and angry because I don't presume to tell other parents what they should be doing. When it's someone I know pretty well, I wait awhile, then confide in them about how advice and criticism make me feel, as if it's a new topic of conversation."

"It's frustrating that parents must endure advice and criticism at such a vulnerable point in their lives, but the worst comes usually with the first child and abates after the second is on its way. I think pregnant women and new parents should wear T-shirts with slogans like: 'I didn't ask so don't tell me. . . .'"

"I try to cultivate friendships, relationships within or without the family circle that build up my confidence in parenting. In this way my resolve is strengthened and I tend not to break down as easily or start to doubt myself because I feel like the only 'oddball.'"

"I carry on just as I am, because I am the mom and have my baby's best interests at heart. After all, it's Parenting from the Heart, no?"

"I must be doing something right. I have a happy, healthy, growing baby—and I'm happy!" ♥

photo courtesy of Melvin and Deborah Fansler

A Nursing Mom's
Holiday Survival Guide

BY ZIPORAH HILDEBRANDT

The holidays are packed with memories and expectations for most of us. With a new family, there is bound to be the added excitement of sharing these special times with your baby, and your baby with your loved ones. Shopping, traveling, hosting parties and visitors, family excitement, school vacations—a lot of moms wish they had two of themselves at this time of year!

How can a nursing mom enjoy the holidays with her baby and stay healthy—and nursing? Here are some suggestions from moms who have lived through the hectic holidays and learned to rise above the stress.

Decide as a family which holidays will be "visiting" holidays and which "home" holidays.

You might decide to spend Hanukkah or Christmas alone at home and visit friends or relatives for a New Year's celebration.

Do less and enjoy it more.

Establish low-stress, close-to-home traditions, such as preparing food together, decorating, singing, and attending a local holiday event. Save the high-energy activities for later years when your kids will better appreciate them.

It isn't necessary to give a great quantity of gifts, especially to very young children. Special time together is as precious as a new toy and will be remembered a lot longer.

Keep shopping, gifts, and celebrations simple and fun. Baking cookies is an activity the youngest children can share and enjoy, and cookies can double as decorations and gifts.

Plan holiday meals that are nutritious as well as special.

Add extras to salads and vegetables, reduce and replace the fat and sugar in baked goods with applesauce, and watch your caffeine intake. Choose healthier desserts, like homemade pumpkin pie and gingerbread. Pass on the candy—serve nuts and dried fruits instead.

Take extra good care of yourself.

Make it a priority to maintain exercise routines. This is not the time to start a strenuous exercise program, but do continue with your usual activity, even when traveling. Besides helping you feel your best and burning off those extra treats, it can give you precious time alone, or a break from crowded homes and family pressures.

At a time when you may be called upon to do extra cooking, it's easy to forget about your own nutritional needs. Instead of sugary decorated cook ies, bake oatmeal cookies packed with wheat germ, nuts, and raisins and sweetened with honey.

It's especially important to get enough sleep. Do your decorating, wrapping gifts, housecleaning, and partying in the earlier hours. Once you're run down, it's hard to catch up. Accept offers to pitch in with cooking and dishes so you can spend time nursing your child.

Reduce stress in any way you can.

Now is a good time to get your holiday nursing wardrobe together. Buying two or three festive nursing tops or dresses in advance eliminates the stress of trying to pull something together at the last minute.

If you have a distance to travel, fly, if possible. Whether you fly or drive, time your departure to miss the worst holiday traffic. Your trip will be shorter, you'll have more energy for your arrival, and your baby will have an easier time.

If you are away from home overnight, be sure you have a place of your own to set out your belongings, feel at home, and nurse in peace.

Try to maintain as much of your baby's routine as possible, especially when it comes to sleep. You won't be relaxed and happy if she isn't.

Cut back on responsibilities you've shouldered in the past. This is the time to let your family know that you have some special needs. Ask for help.

At big family get-togethers there are many eager and loving arms to hold your little one. This can be a blessing for you, but do pay attention to your child's cues about when he needs the security of your familiar arms.

Missing a few parties and family gatherings one year is really not as important as the special relationship you have with your child. You'll have other years to enjoy holiday festivities, but only this time with your baby.

To be sure you'll enjoy the full holiday season, pay special attention to good breastfeeding techniques.

•Be sure your baby is positioned properly for nursing. Read *Bestfeeding: Getting Breastfeeding Right for You*, go to a La Leche League meeting, or call Motherwear for a copy of our free publication "Successful Nursing" for tips on positioning.

•Make sure your bra and clothing do not constrict your breasts in any way. Don't wear tight special-occasion clothes. Wear a nursing bra rather than sliding a regular bra up to nurse.

•Nurse frequently to prevent plugged ducts, breast infections, and premature weaning.

•Rest, sleep, and eat nutritious meals so you don't get run down.

•Relax and enjoy the holidays, and keep nursing your baby! ♥

photo courtesy of the Smith-Bovés

Our Little Lamb Is a Goat

BY CAROL HUBBARD HOUSE

Our little lamb is a goat. I am not talking about some weird permutation of animal husbandry. The subject of this description is a six-month-old Homo sapiens named Benjamin, who is adored by his parents even though his babyhood promises to age them prematurely.

Never mind what the books say about babies fitting into schedules, sleeping through the night, taking a certain number of naps per day, or loving particular foods. Ben's idea of time management is one that changes from week to week, and he successfully resists any and all attempts at manipulating him. He cannot understand why anyone would want to sleep more than four hours at a stretch. Since each day is unique, he believes that the frequency and duration of daily naps must be flexible. At five months of age, he reluctantly acquiesced to the addition of cereal to his diet, but "traditional baby favorites" such as mashed banana and apple juice might as well have been Limburger cheese and vinegar.

Until Benjamin was four months old, I had never heard of "lambs and goats." I was convinced I was a failure as a mother. Somewhere along the line (most likely in the hospital), I had missed a crucial indoctrination session in which new mothers were solemnly instructed in certain vital secrets of parenting designed to produce cooing, contented, and cooperative infants.

It was a chance meeting in the supermarket with an out-of-touch acquaintance that reassured me I hadn't missed any special training. Jean oohed and aahed over Benjamin as he reposed on top of a baby quilt in the child seat of the shopping cart. The pacifier I had judiciously popped into his protesting mouth a few minutes before was still having its intended (albeit short-lived) effect.

"What a little love!" Jean bubbled. "So quiet and sweet! Is he always like this?"

"Well. . ." I hesitated. (I didn't want to sound unloving or unappreciative of our little cherub.) "He's a sweet baby, but he is quite, uh . . . feisty. We really love him," I hurried to assure Jean, "but Ben has the most incredible scream. I'm worn out by the end of the day!"

I peered cautiously out of the corner of my eye at Jean, fearing disapproval or—even worse—that patronizing look that some "veteran" mothers are so fond of casting at us rookies. Instead, I found Jean grinning at me merrily, amusement and perfect comprehension registering clearly on her face.

"Why, honey, you have a little goat!" she chortled.

"A—a what?" I faltered.

"A goat," my new mentor explained cheerfully. "There are lambs and there are goats in the baby world. Our first child, Nathan, is a goat." (I remembered Nathan: a blond toddler with the face of a Botticelli angel and a continual, calculating gleam of mischief in his eyes.)

"I never take Nathan to the grocery store," continued Jean. "I tried it once when he was two months old. He screamed all the way through the store. On the other hand, Dickie, our new baby, is a lamb. I can leave him in his crib cooing at the mobile, come back to him an hour later, and find him still babbling away happily."

A minute later, Jean and I parted company. I was dizzy with relief.

"Lambkin!" I gushed contradictorily at Ben, snatching him up delightedly.

"I'm not a bad Mommy after all—you're just a little goatling!"

Benjamin gave me a very gratifying, dazzling grin as he realized that, at least for the moment, he would be able to view the supermarket world from a vertical position.

In the two months since that fortuitous marketplace encounter, my parental wisdom has mushroomed as I have kept my eyes and ears open for further data on lambs and goats. All my observations continued to confirm the validity of Jean's simple system of classification.

Friends from our Lamaze class, Deb and Mark, have a five-month-old lamb named David. Early discussions with Deb left me feeling very depressed. David only required feedings every three to four hours, and he slept through the night from two months of age. Benjamin, however, decided within the first month that starvation was imminent unless he was nursed every one-and-a-half to two hours during the day and at least three times at night, and he was quick to follow through with his indefatigable, crystal-shattering scream unless I complied promptly.

"Let him cry for two or three nights," the pediatrician advised. "Then he'll learn to get himself back to sleep." (The pediatrician, who has one child of distinctly lambish character, has never heard Ben scream.)

"Oh yes," my friend Patty agreed. "That's what I did with Teddy (an eight-month-old lamb), and it only took two nights!"

"Two nights?" I quavered. "Wasn't it pretty awful?"

"Oh no," she assured me. "I even fell asleep after the first fifteen minutes or so."

This was incomprehensible to me until my husband, Larry, and I took a turn in our church's nursery one Sunday. The aforementioned Teddy was in attendance. After an altercation with another baby, he started to cry. I saw why his mother had told her story so blithely. Three adult workers were conversing in normal tones while one of them rocked Teddy. He cried for five minutes without disturbing their conversation in the slightest.

The next Sunday, I was called out of church by one of the ushers. Benjamin had started screaming in the nursery and could not be consoled. I was greeted at the nursery door by four pale, trembling workers.

"M-m-my..." one girl whispered in a shaking voice. "I've never heard a baby scream like that. Does he ever do that at home?"

"Every day!" I replied wearily. Four pairs of eyes stared at me incredulously. I decided it wasn't worth explaining, as Ben's shrieks continued to rent the air.

There are other significant differences between lambs and goats besides those involving vocal decibel levels and feeding schedules. Lambs sleep wherever they happen to be when the mood hits. Bounce chairs, swings, playpens, department store strollers, a stranger's shoulder—they're all the same to a lamb. Goats, however, insist on sleeping in their own cribs ... and they seldom succumb to the blandishments of the Sandman without putting up a fight.

Lambs will entertain themselves for hours, whether flat on their backs or ensconced in some type of contrivance. If a white wall is all they have to look at, they will stare and smile congenially at it until someone rescues them. But goats have an interest/patience span of one to five minutes, depending on the intrigue value of the nearest object or the imagination of the entertainer.

In the early months, my injudicious complaints about Benjamin's chronic boredom invariably generated enthusiastic testimonials from other parents about wonder devices "guaranteed" to solve my problem. "Get a swing," insisted Sue. "Megan would swing for hours if I kept winding it up. Babies are naturally soothed by motion."

"As soon as Benjamin can sit up well enough to maneuver in a walker, he'll be able to entertain himself for long periods, just like Jeremy does," Anne assured me.

"A bounce chair!" Kate bubbled. "Brian just *loves* bouncing in his while I'm busy around the house!"

"David adores his 'Johnny-Jump-Up,'" declared Bob.

Benjamin, however, quickly taught us that goats seldom "run with the crowd." They generally manage to despise everything that lambs love. As with Tigger in *Winnie the Pooh*, finding out what a goat *does* like requires an exhaustive trial-and-error procedure. Our trial runs with the bounce chair and Johnny-Jump-Up (both fortunately borrowed) were disastrous. To Ben's mind, the former was a jiggling, semi-straitjacket designed to give him headaches, while the latter was a suspension-style device of terror, the only purpose of which was to catapult him willy-nilly from one side of the doorway to the other. The swing and the walker had had their "moments," but never in a predictable manner.

Nevertheless, goats—by their very nature—are captivating. A goat may drive his parents to exhaustion but never to boredom. Benjamin's strong will, spunk, unpredictability, and feistiness are a continual challenge to our patience and creativity, but Larry and I are fond of reminding each other: "such is the stuff of which world movers are made!"

I'm glad Benjamin is a goat. While I'm grateful he wasn't born when I was twenty (and too self-centered and impatient), it's a good thing I didn't wait until my forties (my energy level would never have been sufficient). At thirty, I'm both young enough and old enough to roll with the punches.

Yes, our little lamb is a goat. But reach to pick him up, two dimpled arms fling themselves onto my shoulders; a wet, rosy-mouthed face buries itself in my neck; and a squeal of glee and exuberance bursts from the sturdy little body that I hug as tightly as I dare. That's when I remind myself . . . our little goat is a lamb! ♥

photo courtesy of Sydney Keyes Thackeray

photo courtesy of the Coopers

Sleep

Before becoming parents, you probably took sleep largely for granted. The sun went down, you finished the evening's tasks and activities—washing the dishes, walking the dog, visiting friends, reading a book—and you crawled into bed for a solid night's sleep.

Life has changed. If you're like most parents of a baby, you're spending at least part of your evening singing, rocking, nursing, reading aloud—maybe even driving around the block. And that's just the beginning.

Sleeping from "good night" to "good morning" is not a given. Night nursings, diaper changes, colicky screams . . . . "When will it end?" you groan. One thing is certain: the next night of uninterrupted sleep will not soon be forgotten!

How Does Your Baby Sleep?

BY JODY WRIGHT

Three of my friends have come to me in the last few weeks and asked me whether it was okay that their babies didn't sleep through the night. They were each getting pressured by family and friends to leave their babies to cry in order to "train" them. Each of them referred to books and TV shows that stressed how parents should teach their children to sleep through the night, and that not doing so would cause life-long harm.

I remember this well. As soon as people stopped asking me how much my first baby weighed at birth, they began asking me whether she slept through the night. She didn't, and yours probably doesn't either, but our culture makes a big deal about "good" babies, who sleep all night and don't fuss much, and "fussy" babies who wake up parents and have a lot to say about how they're feeling.

So I read *Solve Your Child's Sleep Problems*, by Richard Ferber, M.D. In my first reading of the book there was little I could pin down that I radically disagreed with, but I felt that the author was suggesting that babies are born bad and we have to train them to become what we want them to be.

I have found that children are very sincere beings who are striving to get their needs met. If we as parents do everything we can to fulfill their deep needs for love, security, and touch, then they naturally want to blend into our lives (night and day!), and into society.

Dr. Ferber bases his book on the premise that babies and children should be able to go to sleep by themselves and should sleep in their own rooms by six months of age. My studies of the human need for touch and of children raised in other cultures indicate to me that humans are meant to sleep with one another, and that human milk should be consumed every few hours, even during the night. Children eventually fall asleep on their own and sleep well if their needs for security and affection have been well met.

Your baby knows what he needs in terms of your presence and your touch. Listen, do your best to fulfill those needs, and he or she will become truly independent when the time is right.

It is natural for your newborn baby to want to sleep right next to you, to hear your familiar sounds and feel the warmth of your body. When she begins to stir, she listens for your slow, steady breathing; soon the rhythm of her breathing will coincide with yours. If you are nursing, you may wake a minute or two before she does, because somehow your sleep cycles have become synchronized. Is it hormones, proximity, or some mystical mothering instinct?

In a few weeks she will be able to sleep without your constant presence, perhaps with just your nightgown left behind to comfort her with your sweet smell. As the months pass, your child will wake less at night and go back to sleep more easily. Teething or fears may interrupt sleep for a time, but be as patient as you can. Introduce your child to new ways of comforting. Sing to him while you nurse, and soon your singing will soothe and lull him when you are not nursing. Hold his hand while he falls asleep. Tell an older child soothing stories that can be the material for sweet dreams.

When your child has weaned herself, just holding your hand can help her center, relax, and go to sleep. And there will come a time when your child will say, "I don't want you to hold my hand, just be here, okay?" And then the night comes that you are very busy, and by the time you get to your child's bedside a sweet, relaxed smile is playing on her sleeping lips.

I know that lovingly fulfilling your children's nighttime needs works, because I had two very fussy babies who, by age four, had become wonderful sleepers. I still hear, "Mom, are you there?" at night sometimes. I answer, "Here I am, everything's okay," and my seven-year-old's breathing becomes deep and long again. My four-year-old slips off her bunk in our family sleeping room and crawls in with Dad a few nights a week. My two-year-old rustles the covers and whispers, "Mama, nursie please," and snuggles with me for a few minutes.

Yes, it's true that I have rarely slept completely through the night in the last seven years. I don't mind at all. I see no fear, no dawdling at bedtime; I see instead the steady maturing of three blossoming children. I feel good about being able to be there for them any time they need me.

It seems much easier to change my own perceptions about where everyone should sleep, when each of us should sleep, and what I can give of myself, than to change the very basic instincts of a child. Throw out all your preconceptions about sleep and do what fulfills your family's needs! ♥

Uncovering the Myths
About Shared Beds

BY BETH HERSH

When I was pregnant with my first child, three different people offered me cribs. I knew for certain that I didn't want the baby in a crib in another room, but beyond that I was unaware of my options.

At my first La Leche League meeting I was handed a copy of Tine Thevenin's priceless book, *The Family Bed*. I read it that night, and my husband read it the next. Since then, three children have been raised in *our* family bed.

Little more than a century ago family sleeping was practiced exclusively in our society for reasons of safety, warmth, and space. The shift to setting up cribs in isolated bedrooms came as a result of larger homes, better heating systems, and a changing psychology regarding child-rearing.

The idea of sleeping with children, now unfamiliar to many Westerners, is practiced in other cultures throughout the world. The importance of loving touch cannot be overrated. It has been proven to be a vital way of helping children develop a sense of themselves as whole, worthwhile, and loved human beings. This need does not vanish in the hours that we are asleep. Even then we are aware, on some level, of what is happening around us.

Children especially, with their fragile bloom of self-esteem, need this level of contact. Dr. Ashley Montagu's work and the wisdom of experienced parents tell us that children who sleep with their parents or with their siblings are freer about showing their affection and have a greater ability to empathize with other family members. This leads to fewer harsh words and misunderstandings and, in my family, an amazing number of spontaneous hugs. As Tine Thevenin puts it so eloquently, "For an average of eight hours, in the stillness of the night, and the relaxing and disarming state of sleep, those that sleep together touch as if to say, 'You are all right. I'm all right. We remain in touch with one another.'"

photo courtesy of Sheree and Eric Barrell

The Family Bed is also filled with practical "how to" advice for setting up shared sleeping. It addresses typical parent concerns with sensible solutions and describes many logical ways to get everyone comfortable in one room.

Though at times having our children with us at night hasn't been easy, we have never regretted it. After spending a night soothing a restless child with a touch and hearing the steady breathing of my toddler so close to my ear, I know it is the right decision for us. And when I wake in the morning and see the clear, bright eyes of my dear baby gazing at me in peace and adoration, I know she has just spent the night in the most perfect place: her family's bed. ♥

Does She Sleep
Through the Night?

BY JUDI HAMMETT

It's inevitable. A new mother takes her baby out into the world, and they're the center of attention. Happy and confident in the spotlight, Mom is suddenly hit with The Question: "Does she sleep through the night?"

I started hearing The Question when my daughter, Maia, was just two months old. My mother raised it first; she was soon joined by the pediatrician, friends, and even people I barely knew. People proudly told me how their babies slept through the night almost from the beginning. Others were quick to offer sympathy or tell me it would be "heaven" when Maia gave me a night of uninterrupted sleep. Absolute strangers advised me to make my tiny girl "cry it out" until she "learned" to sleep through. Clearly this Question was some measure of how good my baby was—and how good a mother I was.

Maia's eight months old now and has never slept through the night. A nightmare? Hardly. Sure, she wakes me up every night—sometimes two or three times—but it's not a problem. This may sound strange, but I know she's not meant to sleep through the night yet.

Maia's early weeks were hard, I'll admit. She cried piteously during our clumsy middle-of-the-night diaper changes, and it was frustrating trying to get her to latch onto the breast properly and stay awake long enough to nurse. Sometimes she couldn't settle down after nursing, so her father and I took turns patting, rocking, and crooning to her until she either calmed down or wanted to nurse again.

After she got the hang of nursing and falling asleep, I had a different problem. Sitting up in bed breastfeeding, I often dozed off. By the time I woke up, put Maia in her cradle, and snuggled under the covers, she needed me again. I made it harder by watching the clock, estimating how much sleep I'd had, how long I'd spent nursing and soothing her, and how much sleep I might get before I had to do it all over again. Something had to change.

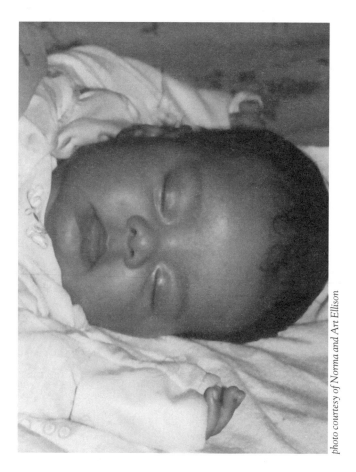

photo courtesy of Norma and Art Ellison

With lots of practice and some strategically placed pillows, I learned to nurse lying down. To avoid nighttime diaper changes, I put two cloth diapers on her at bedtime. I also made myself keep the light off and ignore the clock. Without all that light and activity, it became easier for us both to settle down.

I was amazed at how easy things got. I felt perfectly rested most mornings, no matter how many times Maia needed me. I woke almost before she cried for me, and drifted back to sleep easily as she nursed. Sometimes I wasn't sure how often she'd nursed, as I didn't fully awaken.

Once I learned to cope comfortably with my nighttime responsibilities, my whole attitude changed. I decided to let Maia show me when she was ready to sleep through the night. I felt a crucial part of parenting was following her cues, so I didn't worry that Maia continued to nurse at night as the months passed.

As a first-time mother, it might have been easy for me to doubt my instincts. Many experts insist a baby over three months doesn't need to nurse at night. One popular book actually called my baby's night nursing "a greedy habit." Another said an "improper feeding schedule" made her wake at night. I was supposed to put Maia down to sleep and let her cry. I questioned why I should ignore my baby's cries, and why anyone even cared if she slept through the night.

The Womanly Art of Breastfeeding, by La Leche League International, says this Question only became important because of the inconvenience of bottle feeding at night. Dr. William Sears's *Nighttime Parenting* cites a study showing that breastfed infants wake at night more than formula-fed infants. If more mothers breastfed, perhaps we wouldn't expect babies to sleep through the night.

I also read that as a "constant contact" species, with milk low in protein and fat, we are meant to keep our young close and feed them frequently. Mothers in traditional cultures do exactly this, and consider night nursing completely normal. A study in West Nigeria showed that babies as old as ten months received up to 25% of their milk at night. And some mothers in our own culture even find it normal to nurse toddlers at night, as noted in a recent issue of La Leche League's *New Beginnings* magazine.

I've learned a lot since Maia's birth. I've learned that "experts" can be wrong, and that what we think we know about babies might not be so. Mostly I've learned to trust her instincts, and mine. I'm committed to giving her what she needs, and have not found that to be nearly as difficult as I had anticipated. I'm in no hurry for Maia to sleep through the night, because I know it will happen when the time is right.

I won't say that every night with Maia is a joy. We've had our difficult nights. One night when she was six weeks old and I was sure I had this nighttime stuff down, we were up from 12:30 to 5 A.M. I never did figure out what that was all about. Since then, we've had teething, colds, ear infections, and occasions when Maia thinks 4:30 A.M. is playtime.

I've learned to look for the causes of her nighttime restlessness. Is she getting sick? Does something hurt? Does she need more active play during the day? Does she want to watch TV? (No joke, this did the trick more than once!) I try to respond with patience and a sense of humor. I can't rush Maia from this stage to the next. But I can do what is best for both of us, and try to meet her needs as they arise.

I may even miss her night waking someday. When she nurses in the middle of the night, I don't always fall asleep right away. I lie awake feeling her warm little body cuddled against mine, hearing cute gulping and swallowing sounds in the darkness. All over the world other mothers and babies are doing the same thing, as they have for untold generations. Someday my baby will be a baby no longer, and this will be only a sweet memory. ♥

photo courtesy of Tracie Fore

Mothers Share: Our readers discuss
Sleep Patterns

COMPILED BY JODY WRIGHT

My nine-year-old sleeps mainly in her own room, but she occasionally joins us for part of a night. My seven-year-old sleeps most nights on her mattress on the floor of our room. I built a king-size platform bed a month or so ago, and my mother made us a ruffle and matching curtains in a restful floral pattern. The children's mattresses slip under the bed during the day when my "bedroom elf," our seven-year-old, comes in and straightens. Liina, at five, still sleeps with my husband Prakash and me.

One thing I have noticed about this very gradual, child-initiated independence at night is that the children don't seem to have nightmares. When you share sleep with others, you don't have to worry about waking up scared and having no one there. Bedtime is a very easy time at our house.

Mothers Share asked: What are your baby's sleeping patterns and how does your family solve any related problems?"

"We just had twins, and they are on different sleep schedules. We also have a two-year-old whose sleeping patterns were interrupted, and we found that he just wanted us to be with him. My husband goes in and lies down with him until he falls asleep. It seems sometimes as if it is going to be like this forever. God keeps reminding us that they are young for such a short time, so we don't mind the sacrifice."

"I think our baby at six months sleeps quite well! She usually takes a good morning nap—2 or 3 hours—and sleeps from 10 PM to 8 AM. We just go with the flow and try not to get upset by variations in this pattern. With enough play time and an outing, she is usually tired at the end of the day. She is still sleeping in our room—although we did move her to her crib at about three months after I felt we'd all sleep better apart!"

"I have yet to solve my 'night-owl baby' problem and am looking forward to some suggestions on how to change his habits."

"Hannah (nine months) sleeps two or three times in a day, about 40 minutes each time. I have been nursing her four or five times in a 24-hour period—I love it so!—so it isn't uncommon for her to choose a nap at a nursing session. At night she usually awakens once for a change, some milk, and a kiss or two. She has recently been sleeping straight through, so I have no problems, blessed be!"

"My first child—a girl—started sleeping eight hours a night at three weeks of age. She breastfed like wildfire when she was awake! She weaned herself at fourteen months. My second child—a boy—was three weeks early and a real sleeper at first. Then he started cutting teeth and hasn't slept through the night since he was eight months old, and that was five months ago! We have tried soothing music, Panadol, Orajel, and even letting him 'cry it out,' (our pediatrician's recommendation). I have finally just accepted his sleeping habits and try to nap during the day."

"After the first eight weeks, Matthew (seven months now), slept eight or nine hours a night, a blessing for us. But now on the three evenings I work I awaken him at 12:30 or 1 A.M. for a brief feeding, during which he falls back asleep. The pediatrician told me I could start skipping those feedings, but *he* has never come home from work with full breasts! I feed the baby one breast, pump the other, and then am comfortable and he is satisfied. I also get to change his diaper and to reassure him that Mom is near.

"At $4\frac{1}{2}$ months, when he began waking at 3 AM to feed, I started him on solids during the day, and that seemed to 'cure' him of nocturnal awakening. But now with teething he has been generally more and more irritable and has awakened several nights. I have resorted to bringing him into bed with us. I don't even change him; I just bring him in, let him nurse and fall asleep, and return him to his crib."

"I have tried but have not been able to sleep the night with the baby in the bed. He seems to wake more often this way. Then we all awake intermittently through the night. I take Matt into our bed at midday for his nursing and nap. If I can't sleep with him (at least I get some shut-eye), I wrap his arms around a teddy bear, leaving him on his side. I then sneak out of the bed and cover him with a blanket."

"At thirteen months, our baby became very sick and passed away within a few weeks. Until the day she was admitted to the hospital, we had a family bed. Elyse also nursed before falling asleep. The arrangement began when Elyse was six months old, outgrew her bassinet, and was given a crib, which she slept in for one week without a problem. We tried all methods to make her sleep there but it became apparent that she preferred to sleep with her parents. As the family bed worked for the three of us (everyone slept at night), we were not deterred by the MANY who felt this was unacceptable. We had Elyse for such a short time that I am very happy we had her sleep with us and nurse even through such disapproval. There are so many uncertainties in life. Opportunities to love and show affection should be seized and not let pass by."

"Andrew was a 'snacky' baby who nursed often and drank only a little at a time, so he woke often at night as he was legitimately hungry. After three weeks of having him sleep in a bassinet in our room, we 'gave in' and brought him into our bed with us. We got a lot more sleep.

"I believe my sleep patterns and his synchronized so that I was in a dreamlike state or even awake as he woke up hungry, so I didn't feel as interrupted as when he woke me from a deep sleep. Also, when he had a cold or slight congestion, I was much more relaxed knowing I would hear him immediately if he was struggling for breath. It kept me from worrying about SIDS.

"Andrew woke up several times every night for months and at least once per night until he turned two. And although he knew it was night and could get himself back to sleep, he would wake up again within thirty minutes if he had not been fed. He truly needed that night feeding! I believe answering his nighttime needs of security, warmth, and nourishment were important in giving him the happy, independent personality he now has. *Nighttime Parenting* by Dr. Sears and *The Family Bed* by Tine Thevenin are excellent resources."

"My daughter is a great sleeper—I think it is because we let her take her naps around the family's activity and have been taking her to bed with us since she was two weeks old. She is a healthy, happy, seven-month-old, totally breastfed baby who hardly ever cries."

"My daughter, at fifteen months, wakes to nurse two or three times a night. I think a family bed helps; it's easy to just roll over. I always end up falling back asleep. I believe that RARE is the baby who sleeps all night. It's important not to buy into this myth and also to just accept waking. With my first, I spent more energy fighting his sleep patterns. To relax and say 'okay, this is it for awhile' really does help."

"I want to share the attitude my husband and I have about our seventeen-month-old's sleeping habits. We've tried hard to take our cues from him, tried not to have adult expectations about how or where or when he should sleep. We've discovered that through loving patience and response, the 'unwanted' wakings at night don't go on forever and that a brief, loving nursing or cuddling at night makes him happy and we also, with the knowledge we've met his needs!"

"Our fifteen-month-old strongly disliked being separated from me from the very beginning. He'd always fall asleep nursing in my arms and most of the time would wake up when I put him down. Although we kept the bassinet, and later a crib, right next to the bed, he was never really content. He slept through the night perhaps twice.

"At about six months, once in the crib, he began to awaken two, three, four times a night to be brought to bed to nurse. Many times I left him in bed with us (I'd fall asleep nursing). He stayed in bed with us more and more. At one point we tried *hard* to get him used to his crib (which his grandparents bought and I did feel obliged to use!). One night he cried for over an hour, and that was the last we ever tried that. It broke my heart.

"From the time he was ten months, we have had a family bed exclusively. My only regret is that I did not do that from the very beginning (although he was often in bed with us). I know now that this is exactly what he wanted and needed and I strongly suspect this is the case with most every baby. Let's all use our obsolete cribs to store baby clothes and stuffed animals! Although we never sleep through the night now, I feel as though we have enough sleep. The baby still wakes up as many as four times a night and needs to nurse to go back to sleep."

"Our youngest is now a little over a year old. He has slept in our bed since birth, and I have managed to get some sleep because of our family bed. My husband sleeps with us some nights, but most often ends up sleeping on the couch because he's such a light sleeper.

"The way that our bedroom is designed, there's no way we can switch the baby to a side-car, bassinet, or bed next to the wall. Our five-year-old has ended up sleeping in the bed with us these past few weeks and always looks forward to it. He sleeps like a rock. I know eventually, probably in another year, I'll move the youngest into his big brother's bed, and then my husband will move back into our bed. He's not crazy about sleeping on the couch but would rather have this than very little sleep. This arrangement doesn't bother me because I always feel rested in the morning after snuggling next to my nursing baby. I must say that my husband is a very patient man."

"Our nine-month-old, Jonathan Aaron, has a soft, plush polar bear (rather large and cuddly) that has been his 'comforter' since the age of six months. Every night I place 'Mr. Bear' near his head in the crib. If Jonathan awakens, he reaches for Mr. Bear and snuggles close—unless he's hungry. Jonathan's room is directly across the hall from ours, so I go to him quickly if/when he cries out. I bring him to bed with me and nurse back to sleep. If he merely fusses for a minute, I know that he is searching for Mr. Bear, and Mr. Bear will help settle him back down quickly. I check on him only to find that he has laid his head on Mr. Bear, draped one arm over his comforting friend, and is sleeping soundly!"

"My son, now eight months, has been sleeping with us since birth. All of us enjoy this; he has never slept in a crib. There are nights when he is up nursing a lot, but I can usually doze while he's nursing. My husband will often snuggle with Alexander, and that helps him to go back to sleep when I am very tired."

"Katie (six weeks), sleeps off and on during the day in her stroller (great for rocking), in her bassinet, or on the bed with me if we take a nap together. She sleeps with us in bed at night. Her baby sling is great for housework and trips! She promptly falls asleep or nurses and then falls into a peaceful sleep.

"Having her sleep in our family bed has been very positive. I get a lot more sleep—nursing lying down, etc. My husband works various shifts, so the family bed has been a godsend for me when he works nights and I have to do everything!"

"My baby is almost one year old and is breastfed. He's not much of a day napper and wakes two to four times a night. During the day I let him nurse on demand, and he falls asleep when he is tired enough. I lay him down in a crib and he naps 15 to 45 minutes. At night he nurses to sleep after a warm tub and again is put into his crib. When he wakes up the first time, he comes into bed with my husband and me. I guess you could call this a 'modified' family bed.

"I used to think this was all a problem until I decided that he just doesn't need as much sleep as I would like him to have. I no longer watch the clock or count the times he wakes at night. I trust he will sleep through the night when he is able to. I'm content now that I've rethought his needs and stopped comparing him to other babies." ♥

photo courtesy of Elisabeth Liebow

Baby's Sleep Needs and You

BY ZIPORAH HILDEBRANDT

Babies are not convenient. Babies have needs that just don't fit neatly into our lifestyles. They need to be held, so we get carriers and car seats to bring them with us. They need special food, so we either buy clothes that help us nurse them or buy formula and bottles to feed them. They need their own bathroom facilities, so we have a system of diapers, covers, and laundry. They need to be with someone all the time, so we hire people to be with them when we can't.

When it comes to sleeping arrangements, many people balk. A crib is the accepted equipment. We spend money to arrange for all the other things—why not just a baby-size bed that a baby can't fall out of? Isn't that what everyone else does? If we're worried that we can't hear the baby's cries, we can get a monitor, right?

Well, maybe. A baby's sleep needs are not as obvious as her other needs. We are so used to sleeping at night and being awake all day that accommodating a baby's different rhythm seems like a hardship. But babies are different. Newborns need to sleep fourteen to eighteen hours a day. Just as they need to eat frequent small meals, newborns need frequent, short naps. Even at night.

There are two kinds of sleep: active sleep and quiet sleep. Active sleep is characterized by rapid eye movement (REM), frequent position shifts, and irregular breathing. During active sleep, it is easy to awaken someone, and easy for the sleeper's own movements, hunger, or other bodily sensations to awaken her. A newborn spends about half of her sleep in active sleep, while an adult spends only about twenty percent of sleep time in this state.

As a baby matures, her brain naturally learns to inhibit the impulse to awaken. She sleeps longer and more restfully and spends more of her time in quiet sleep. But until a baby reaches this stage, she is subject to frequent waking. At first, she wakes from hunger. After a few months, however, other signals awaken her. Chief among those is the need for companionship. It makes perfect sense to be there with her, to nurse, to give warmth and comfort. This is what most cultures throughout history have done. Only in the last hundred years or so have most babies in western cultures been forced into separate beds.

I always had my daughter sleep beside me. She was a difficult, colicky baby, which made it all the more important that she was with me every moment. It was terribly hard waking every half hour to her screams, then rocking, nursing, and patting her back to sleep only to wake again and again. If I'd had to get out of bed, even go into another room, I would have been a much worse wreck than I was. Actually, after the first month, I really didn't feel the lack of sleep. I could sleep while she nursed. My husband and I became adept at patting and rocking without really waking up.

Yes, a child's sleep needs can oppose our own needs for precious moments to ourselves. Someone convinced us once to try the "let her cry" method. What a dismal experience. We only tried it for a short time—minutes of hell as her cries escalated from piercing to heart-rending. I later found out something that justified me in abandoning that unpleasant experiment: When it comes to crying, there are babies who can calm themselves—self-soothers—and there are babies who can't. Self-soothers, left alone, will cry briefly and then find something, like sucking a thumb, that will help them stop. The non-self-soothers, however, just keep on crying and crying until they are screaming and choking—a dangerous situation.

Think about it. There you are, alone and hating it, wanting someone so much and all you can do to call that person is cry. Are you thinking to yourself, "Gosh, my mom and dad have really important things to do right now—the dishes, the laundry, reading the paper—but they still love me and care about me even though they aren't here with me. I guess I'll just go to sleep"? Or are you thinking, "I need someone real badly, and no one's coming even though I'm calling as hard as I can—I'm doing everything I know how to do to get what I need but it isn't working. I've failed. I may as well go to sleep, I'll never get what I need, I've failed!"?

Babies who are left to cry are learning to get to sleep on their own. But they are also learning a lesson of despair and failure. Asking for what they need doesn't work. They're doomed to loneliness and fear. Babies whose parents respond promptly to crying are learning that they matter, they are important and loved, their efforts toward expressing their needs are respected. They learn success.

My family and friends often expressed disbelief at the extent to which I modified (to their minds) my life to accommodate my young daughter's needs. I did not see it that way. To me, my parenting style was the only style that felt right. I believed that meeting all my baby's needs for security and closeness meant she would grow up feeling loved, satisfied, and happy. I have seen nothing to make me doubt that belief, and everything to say that I was right. Sure, it was hard sometimes. There were nights when I desperately wanted some time to myself, when she just would not stay asleep. I would nurse her, she'd fall asleep, but as soon as I tried to take my nipple back she would start sucking again. Or she would wake as soon as I wasn't touching her.

I learned to move gradually, to leave my hand on her back so she'd feel me, to stay seated on the bed for a few minutes beside her, to tuck my warm pillow against her side. Looking back on those years, there are few things I can imagine that could be as sweetly fulfilling as the feeling of my baby's head snuggled against my arm as I awoke in the morning. And nothing can compare to that first radiant smile when she opened her eyes and looked at me. ♥

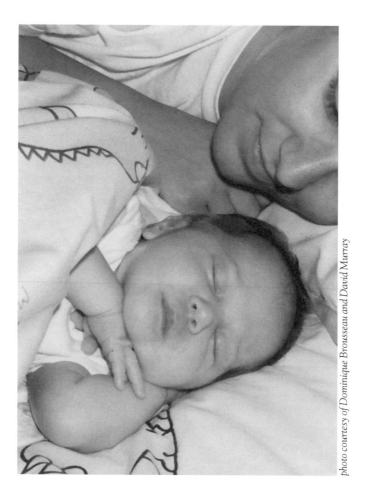

photo courtesy of Dominique Brousseau and David Murray

Lullabies

BY DENISE A. BERG

I knew even before my son David was born that he was a night owl. When I settled myself down to sleep at 10 PM, I began to feel lots of kicks and punches. Just as I began to sleep, he would wake up, and wake me up.

It was no surprise to discover after David was born that he would not necessarily want to sleep when his father and I wanted to sleep. Luckily for us, my mother came to stay for the first week of his life, and we had some aid when we needed our rest very early in the morning.

After Grandmom went home and Dad went back to work, I had to fend for myself in the nighttime hours. That was when I learned the importance of lullabies. David and I had one lullaby between us when we first started out together. It was a little folk piece I had learned from a popular record album many years before. I sang it over and over at 3 A.M. I liked the song and it seemed that David did, too, but one song over and over can soon drive a mother nuts.

Help was on the way, however. My relatives all began to remember songs they hadn't sung in years. They started to sing automatically, and I can tell you, I picked up my ears and listened. These were songs I hadn't heard since my nieces were babies, and songs that were certainly sung to me many years ago.

David was treated to one lullaby at midnight and another one at 2 or 3 A.M. He was still staying awake, but he did lie quietly while I sang. He didn't care if my vocalizing was cracked or off-key. I began to remember little hymns and songs from my childhood with simple words to teach and comfort children. These had short tunes and easy melodies that my groggy brain could handle. David still did not go back to sleep for at least an hour after I fed him. Did he like the music so much? He could now hear several songs in a row as he lay in my arms with his eyes wide open.

When David was about two months old, I found a mail-order offer for a tape of lullabies. Aha, I thought, this should be interesting. One side of the tape had the vocals and the other side instrumentals. It was moderately priced, so I sent for it. It has long since paid for itself. It added several more lullabies to our collection. What's more, I didn't have to sing unless I wanted to. And I finally had the words to *Brahms' Lullaby*—fitting, since half of his musical toys play the melody.

David took four and a half months to "sleep through." In that time, he learned my voice and together we learned a dozen lullabies. They spoke of little things like lambs and stars and angels and babies. They spoke of family and closeness and caring and protection, but mostly they spoke of love. Their words kept me awake and focused as I cared for my son in the low light of nighttime. Their rhythms put him to sleep as I rocked him in time to the music. Now I have a second son. Joseph loves the lullabies, too. I know we are closer because of them, and I'm sure that's why people have sung them from time immemorial. ♥

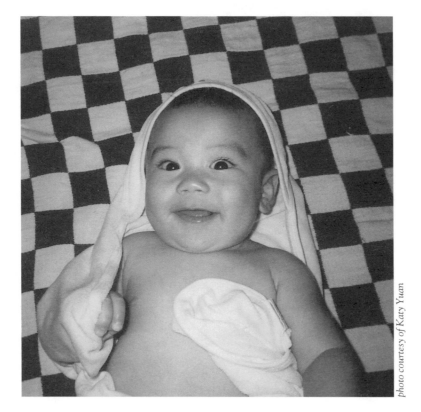

photo courtesy of Katy Yuan

Health and Safety

Most of us would agree that our children's health and safety are absolute priorities. When we breastfeed, we start our children with the healthiest food there is. Along with a perfect balance of nutrients we provide protection from illness and disease and a nurturing bond that is the foundation of sound emotional health.

As our babies grow and their needs change, our roles change, too. We need to give them proper food and clothing, teach them safety, and attend to their well-being in a world where they are exposed to things beyond our control. We must be ever-vigilant, for the first years at least, to set them on a wholesome course. It is so much easier to start them off right than to turn them around once they're on their way.

photo courtesy of the Smith-Bovés

Wholesome Ways
to Feed Your Little One

BY BETH HERSH

I t sounds strange, but I get a real thrill when my children ask for a second helping
of broccoli. It tells me that I have conveyed good eating habits to them and
prepared wholesome food that they enjoy.

When should you start feeding your baby "solid foods"? What should you feed,
in what form? What should you avoid? How can you make sure your baby is getting
what she or he needs? How can you prevent allergies? How can you make all of this
easy for yourself? Starting your baby on solid foods is exciting, but it can also be scary.
We know that our children's health and many of their lifelong eating habits are
affected by our decisions, but there are so many questions when we first start out.
These answers should get you started with confidence.

How do you know when your baby should start solids?

All babies are different. One of mine started solid foods at five months and another not until nine months. According to *The Womanly Art of Breastfeeding*, by La Leche League International, "Breastmilk is the perfect food for at least the first six months for the healthy, full-term infant." When most babies start to teethe—between six and eight months, some earlier, some later—the natural urge to bite and chew begins to develop. At this point, the mouth, tongue, and digestive system are probably ready for solid foods. Watch your baby, not the calendar. If she suddenly wants to be fed more, and increased nursing for four or five days doesn't satisfy her, try starting solids.

The Womanly Art of Breastfeeding goes on to say, "Some babies with a tendency toward allergies will refuse solids even at six or eight months. This could be nature's way of protecting that baby from foods that will cause him problems. Such babies can continue to do well on breastmilk alone until their systems are ready to tolerate other foods." Your main concern should be that your child continues to gain weight. If he doesn't, discuss it with your health-care provider.

What solid foods are best to start with?

Recommended early foods include apple juice, applesauce, avocados, bananas, barley, millet, papaya, pears, rice, sweet potatoes, and yogurt. Soft, easy to digest, unprocessed foods are the best choices. Whatever you are eating has a natural attraction for your baby. Run a spoonful through a grinder and see how it goes.

What shouldn't your baby eat?

According to *The Womanly Art of Breastfeeding*, you should avoid processed foods, because they are often full of sugar, salt, preservatives, and chemicals. *The Natural Baby Food Cookbook* suggests staying away from foods like carrots and string beans until you are sure your baby can handle them, probably after eighteen months of age. The authors further urge: "Do NOT give these small hard foods to any baby under a year old: 1. Raw celery—even for an older child, scrub the celery well and blanch it briefly in boiling water to get rid of the possible contamination of salmonella. 2. Raw peas and string beans. 3. Nuts and peanuts. 4. Whole corn kernels. 5. Popcorn. 6. Whole or unseeded berries. 7. Dry cereal. 8. Hard candies. 9. Potato chips." The information I have collected over the years leads me to suggest that the following foods be put off until after one year: citrus fruits and juices, wheat, eggs, milk products except perhaps cultured ones (e.g., cottage cheese and yogurt), chocolate, shellfish, pork, soy, strawberries, and honey (which has caused concern because its botulism content cannot be processed in the digestive system of babies).

How can you make feeding natural foods to babies easy?
A food grinder, pressure cooker, freezer, blender, etc., make preparing your baby's food a snap. The older your baby is when she starts to eat, the less grinding you will need to do.

Babies love finger foods they can eat themselves, and eating keeps your baby entertained while you go about your kitchen responsibilities. (*Never* leave the room when your baby is eating.) My experience is that the more wholesome and natural the family's diet, the easier it is to prepare food for the baby. All the items are in your meal, and a little forethought ensures that they are taken out for your baby at the right time in the cooking process. With time, you will learn what to keep around—in your bag, your car, and your kitchen—for quick snacks.

How can you prevent allergies?
If you are nursing your baby, you are doing the very best thing you can to prevent the development of allergies, which research often traces back to babyhood. Nurse as completely as possible for as long as possible, and you will be doing much to give your child a healthier life. If you have a family history of allergies, do all you can to understand them and how they work. There are many good books on the subject.

I've never used bottled baby foods or boxed baby cereals. It is really quite easy to feed a baby wholesome foods right from your own kitchen. Once you get the hang of it, a whole new gastronomic world of delicious wholesome food will open up for both of you! ♥

Some Thoughts on Cutting
the Food Budget

BY BETH HERSH

In this world of sky-high costs, things we used to take for granted—gas for the car, a roof over our heads, healthy, interesting foods for the family—have to be thought of in a new way. Not all of these costs can be controlled, but when it comes to your food budget, there *is* some room for juggling. At the same time, this is where you can make positive changes that will benefit your health.

Not long ago, when I realized I would have to cut my food budget, I visualized meal after meal of boring, bland food and the kids just not wanting to eat. That isn't what happened at all. Somehow we were able to pull some ideas together that made eating more of a family experience and more fun. We also made it all much more affordable.

The first thing we did was pay attention to where we shop. I have found food co-ops, where you can usually trade time for goods, to be the best for savings. Being a co-op member sometimes requires a small fee or an hour or two of work every week, but it pays you back in discounts and wholesome foods. Most foods in co-ops are packaged in bulk, so you buy only what you want. You don't pay for the hidden costs of advertising and fancy, eye-catching packages you'd encounter at a supermarket.

Everyone knows it is best not to shop when you're hungry and everything looks and smells irresistible. I would like to suggest that you don't shop when you are feeling needy in any way. The day that everything is going wrong and there doesn't seem to be any relief is not the day to have your senses blasted with an array of high-fat, high-sugar foods. All judgment falls away, and you wind up buying a lot of comfort foods that really do nothing more than set you back on your path to good health (and cutting the food budget!). Sometimes taking a short walk or sitting with your eyes closed before entering a store can give back some of the energy that has been drained out of you, clearing your mind to shop wisely and bear your health in mind.

I like to approach supermarkets with a list of all the things I intend to buy. What you really need at home is usually less expensive than whatever appeals to you as you're pushing a cart up and down the aisles of the market. Also keep in mind that different supermarkets do not charge the same prices. Some have different grades of the same food or a less expensive store brand. And clipping coupons does not necessarily save you money. A coupon is only really worth the discount if you were going to buy the item anyway.

One place I always check at the supermarket is the reduced-price produce rack. While the fruit is often too old to use, the vegetables are usually fine for cooking if you are going to cook them that day. I buy the vegetables that I can't usually afford, like mushrooms, and cook up a double batch of mushroom barley soup or tofu stroganoff. Then I freeze half of it and have a supply for another night that hardly costs me anything.

Another strategy I use for buying vegetables is to buy only what I expect to use that day and maybe the day after. Even though I know that I don't plan to be back at the supermarket for a week, there are lots of farm stands or small produce stores where I can pick up fresh veggies during the week. That way, I never buy more than I can use and I don't wind up composting my money. And since I only buy what I am in the mood for, I really look forward to my meal.

Meal planning is the area where my family has made the most changes. I have found that dressing up a simple meal with one fancy ingredient can make all the difference in how it is received. Grain burgers can be jazzed up with special burger buns. Plain beans can be vitalized with sliced black olives. By making a meal a little bit fancy, the kids really enjoy it.

I believe in food treats. I don't think we need to deprive ourselves of yummy foods and snacks just because we are trying to save money. I always manage to save enough for one extravagance. It can be a pastry, a bit of a special cheese, or a bottle of wine, something that makes me feel I'm being good to myself. My children buy themselves food treats when they shop with me. I have found that when they are holding their treat on the way to the check-out counter, they don't seem to mind that there are no cookies or chips or special cereals in the cart.

The price difference between store-bought cookies and homemade cookies is amazing. I bake lots of cookies at home for after school or lunch-box treats. I have a few simple recipes and endless variations that the kids love. I have to account for the gas I use to bake them, but that helps to heat my house in the winter, and in the summer we turn to other treats. Again, I usually buy one special ingredient, like chocolate chips, to add pizzazz to a basic cookie recipe.

There are a lot of inexpensive snacks that can be great fun for a child. There must be a hundred ways to make popcorn, for example. Sometimes we put on olive oil, cheese, and garlic. Other times we add honey and nuts. The variations are endless, and each feels like a new treat.

When I go out with the kids, it's easy to spend a lot of money on food. I have learned never to set foot out the door without packing a snack unless I know we will only be gone for a short while. The snack can be as simple as peanut butter and jelly sandwiches or a few carrot sticks. Hungry kids need food, and if I don't bring something, I have to buy something.

Along the same lines, I got out of buying the individual juice cartons by getting each child a special cup with a top and straw. They are every bit as satisfied with their special system for transporting juice as they would be with the little boxes. Once in a while, I buy a couple boxes on sale or for when the kids are sick. Juice boxes become ultimate treats.

When I take my kids out to eat, we often don't have a full meal. I have learned to zero in on what will comprise a real treat and go straight for that. We eat the rest of the meal at home.

These are some of the ways my family saves money. Food doesn't have to be expensive to be good. Investigate some of the programs in your area for low-income families such as Food Stamps, WIC, or food banks. A little help can go a long way. I have also learned to accept gifts of food: produce from a neighbor's garden or casseroles and soups made by friends. I give the same when I am able. I give groceries to many food drives and shelters, and sometimes I stand outside supermarkets to help collect. In many ways, we all must feed one another. ♥

photo courtesy of the Zimmermans

Learning About Homeopathy

BY MICHELE SELLNER PAINE

I must admit that when I first heard of homeopathic medicine, I was a skeptic. If I had never heard of it before, I asked myself, how could it be legitimate? An article in *Parenting From the Heart* explained a few of the basics, but I still wasn't sold. Then one Sunday evening last spring, my one-year-old son, Tyler, awoke with a distressing fever. He screamed in discomfort. When I picked him up he cried even harder. It was midnight, a long time until the doctor's office opened.

With the underlying feeling of uncertainty that all parents have when a child is sick, we proceeded to administer acetaminophen, the only medicinal help we could offer him. He resisted the bitter, burning liquid and promptly vomited what we did force into him. At this point my husband and I felt utterly helpless, and we spent a long night waiting for the doctor's assistance.

I began to think about this helplessness. I longed for something that would enable me to provide relief for my child. Because a fever is the body's way of fighting infection, it seemed that the logic behind pain and fever relievers was backward. I vowed to learn more about alternatives, since the things I knew and practiced only frustrated me. I ordered a copy of *Homeopathic Medicine at Home*, by Maesmund B. Panos, figuring that its eight-dollar price would be offset by the next bottle of acetaminophen I would not have to buy.

The early chapters of the book relate the history and principles of homeopathy. Homeopathic medicine is based on the principle that like will cure like. If a person encounters symptoms of muscle aches and pains, for instance, the remedy of choice would be Arnica, for when this substance is given to a healthy person in large doses, these same symptoms occur.

Unlike allopathic medicine, there is no single remedy for any given ailment. Shortly after I invested in a home remedy kit, my husband brought my son home from daycare with a cold. Unfamiliar with homeopathic medicine, Dad simply looked for a bottle that read "colds" and administered a dose. He failed to read the book, which details the signs, conditions, and complaints of the patient that guide you to a homeopathic diagnosis. Fortunately, homeopathic remedies carry no side effects; if the remedy is wrong, there will simply be no improvement, an indication to reassess the symptoms and try another remedy.

One weekend, Tyler woke up vomiting and suffering from diarrhea. Since he was thirsty for cold water and had a fever, I administered Phosphorus. His vomiting stopped, and his fever went down. When he vomited again after his afternoon nap, I gave him another dose and the symptoms once again ceased. He was able to keep down liquids and crackers after that.

When he returned to daycare the following Monday, the caregiver noted that other toddlers had come down with this same flu, only it seemed to last about a week. She wondered what I gave him that stopped the vomiting and diarrhea so quickly. When I told her I gave Tyler a homeopathic remedy, she looked confused, but I walked away feeling satisfied that homeopathy did work, and yes, I knew how to use it.

Pioneer women often relied upon homeopathy for their families' illnesses, for doctors were scarce. Homeopathic medicine is used by the British royal family, and is widely accepted in Europe. Homeopathy works equally well on adults, babies, and animals. But the reaction of my son's caregiver is not unusual. Even my pediatrician did not seem to know much about the practice.

I have gradually developed a faith in this natural form of medicine. It is unlike conventional medicine, which leads us to believe that the right chemicals or procedures can cure any illness. Homeopathy takes time to learn, and it is sometimes frustrating to have to look at all the facets of a sickness. My husband once got angry with me for asking him so many questions about his condition, but it has gotten easier. Now my whole family is benefiting from homeopathy, and my confidence as a competent parent is growing. I can finally throw away the acetaminophen and prescribe natural substances that really work. ♥

photo courtesy of Tanya and Bill Weiss

The Healing Team

BY BETH HERSH

There is no one who knows your child better than you do. You know how she acts when she is happy and how her behavior changes when something is bothering her. You know all the subtle signs, from a slight paleness to outright tears, both on the obvious and the intuitive levels. You can sense, often before the child herself can, when there is something wrong, either physical or emotional. Then, with some cuddling and appropriate questions, you can usually get the information you need to begin the work of healing.

This very personal knowledge is vital in maintaining your child's health. Unfortunately, it is often overlooked by medical professionals in their belief that they possess all the information necessary to get your child well. Because of their extensive training and their very real knowledge of symptoms and diseases, they often overlook the value of the intimate knowledge that parents have of their children.

It is when the parent and the doctor each recognize their valuable positions and are able to communicate their unique information to each other that a healing team is formed. This team, by keeping the lines of respect and communication open, is far more powerful than either one working alone.

I have a friend whose child was born with spina bifida, a condition where the spine is open and the vital spinal fluid is unable to flow freely. What doctors do in this case is insert a shunt, a tube that allows the spinal fluid to flow from the brain to where it is needed. If this shunt becomes blocked or malfunctions in any way, spinal fluid can build up in the brain, causing irreparable damage. In my friend's case, she began to realize that Mara was not feeling well. Through her knowledge of the condition and her very real intuitive knowledge of her daughter, she was able to determine that the shunt was partially blocked.

She took this information to her doctor who then did all the tests that might determine if there was a blockage. The tests came back negative. He scheduled Mara for surgery primarily on the basis of her mother's observations. He believed in the value of the knowledge of the mother. In fact, there was a blockage in the shunt that eventually would have shown up in one of the tests. By clearing it out before it became severe enough to be evident in the testing process, it is possible they saved Mara from further damage—even paralysis. In this case, parent and doctor pooled their knowledge and resources and were able to give the very best care to the child.

A third component of the healing team, and no less important, is the child herself. A child who is able to tell you where it hurts and how it feels makes any diagnosis much easier and more accurate. Teaching children how the systems of the body work and helping them to be aware of what they are feeling and how to verbalize it, are very important lessons. Children who are aware of their feelings will be more in tune with their bodies. They may even be able to prevent some illnesses by recognizing the very early signs and learning the treatments for them.

Healing, becoming well and remaining well, is a process of getting information and making knowledgeable decisions about what action to take. There is no one member of the team who is any more vital than any other, because each has information the other needs to make the most informed choices about care. When parents know that no one knows their child as they do, when the child knows that she is really being heard, and when doctors realize that their information is limited because it is general and not yet specific to that child, then the real healing team is formed. Then mutual trust and respect can develop. The result is not just the healing of an acute illness, but a pattern that can be continued for a lifetime. ♥

photo courtesy of Denise Evarts

Protecting Kids from the Sun

BY ZIPORAH HILDEBRANDT

If a child in Australia arrives at school without a hat, she or he is sent home. Australia is the closest continent to Antarctica, home of the largest hole in the ozone. Sun protection for children is taken very seriously there because a single severe sunburn before age eighteen is thought to double the risk of melanoma, the most serious form of skin cancer. Children's skin is much more vulnerable to harm from burning than adults', and most children spend much more time in the sun.

The ozone layer is deteriorating faster than anyone thought. That means more UV (ultraviolet) radiation reaches the earth. Ninety percent of skin cancers have been linked to UV radiation. The EPA predicts twelve million additional cases of skin cancer in the next forty years—and those victims are kids now. The rate of melanoma has doubled in less than ten years. It is the number-one cancer in women under thirty-five, and increasing rapidly. Scary? You bet.

Teach your kids to protect themselves. Set a good example. Wear tightly woven hats and shirts, use sunscreen, and play in the shade even on cloudy days. Try to find indoor activities during midday when UV is most intense. Teach kids the "shadow test": if your shadow is shorter than you are, stay out of the sun.

Sunscreen may be our best defense against skin cancer, but it is no panacea.

Be sure to get a sunscreen that protects both UVA and UVB radiation. And don't use sunscreen as an excuse to spend more time in the sun. The increased incidence of skin cancer is linked to sunscreen use as well as the deterioration of the ozone.

Be especially careful with your kids and sunscreen. Some chemicals are irritating to sensitive skin, and experts advise against using sunscreen on babies under six months. They advise that infants be kept entirely out of the sun and wear broad-brimmed hats outdoors.

Test a sunscreen on your child's arm and wait a day or two. If there is irritation or redness, try a different formulation. Look for formulas free of alcohol, fragrance, colors, PABA, and carrot seed oil. Ingredients such as aloe vera gel, vitamin E, cocoa butter, and fatty acids will moisturize, heal, and protect. Water-resistance is a must, so your youngster can splash safely for up to forty minutes before reapplying.

A sunscreen's SPF (Sun Protection Factor) is a rating based on its ability to block UVB: the burning, short UV wavelengths. With an SPF of 15 or higher, there will also be *some* protection from the longer UVA wavelengths that cause long-term damage. If you figure the minimum time it takes you to burn when unprotected at noon in summer, then multiply the number of minutes by the SPF, you will know how long an application will protect you. If you burn in 30 minutes, for example, an SPF 8 sunscreen will protect you for four hours, an SPF 20 for ten hours. You can burn through your clothes, too. A poly/cotton shirt has an SPF of 16, light all-cotton tees are SPF 8. If you can see through it, UV can go through it. Choose tight weaves and light colors for the best protection.

The nearer the equator you go and the higher above sea level, the faster you'll burn. Consider this when you choose a sunscreen.

Remember—the chemicals that protect your skin have to first be absorbed by your skin. Apply a liberal amount of sunscreen *at least thirty minutes* before exposure to the sun; an hour is even better. Rub it in well and reapply frequently. Reapplication doesn't extend the time you are protected; it merely renews the protection you have. For longer protection, you have to get a higher SPF.

Many drugs make skin and eyes more sensitive to light, including tetracycline and some other antibiotics, antihistamines, coal and tar derivatives (for instance dandruff shampoos), some oral contraceptives, ibuprofen, antidepressants, and anti-nausea drugs. If you're taking medication, check with your doctor. Taking supplemental zinc, beta-carotene, and vitamins A and E can help your skin, eyes, and immune system (and your nursing child) deal with the sun's damage.

We all love the sun, and it can only help to we use common sense, proper clothing, and appropriate sunscreens. ♥

photo courtesy of Diana Norman

Dressing Your Baby
for Cold Weather

BY ZIPORAH HILDEBRANDT

Young babies cannot regulate their own temperature; they need you to do it for them. Not only are their systems immature, but their skin has no subcutaneous layer of fat for insulation. Since their bodies are so small compared to the surface area of their skin, they lose proportionally more body heat than adults.

Babies' metabolisms are faster than ours to support their incredible growth rate; they burn calories much more quickly. Their caloric intake needs to be higher in proportion to their size, as well. And since those stomachs are so tiny, babies need to nurse more frequently in cold weather. If a baby has to burn her precious blood sugar keeping warm, she can't use those calories for growth. This is one reason that feeding on demand is so important. Your baby knows when she needs food!

Newborns who are kept warm are less likely to be jaundiced, and also less likely to suffer from diarrhea. They prefer a temperature in the 80s. (Infant massage practitioners know that in a cool room, all the babies will fuss until the room warms up!)

Babies fuss for lots of reasons, some of which we'll never know. But there is a short list of "firsts" to consider: is he hungry? Wet? Sleepy? No? Then try adding a hat, booties, another layer, or a blanket. Layer buntings on top of shirts and pants. The length reduces the chances of tummy exposure when a baby is picked up or carried and protects against drafts on the floor. Remember that the air on the floor is cooler than at couch or head level, where grown-ups feel it. Get a cozy quilt or a wool pad to put your baby on.

How can you tell how much clothing a baby needs? First, notice what you are wearing. Your baby will need that much, plus or minus. If you are exercising, and your baby is not, your baby will need more clothing. If your baby is in a stroller, where more of him is exposed to air and wind, he'll need more layers and extra protection for hands, feet, and head. If he's crawling, running, or walking, he may need a layer of clothing taken off. This is one reason dressing babies in layers works so well. The layers also trap warm air between them, acting as the extra insulation babies don't have.

Don't underestimate the chill of the wind. A winter wind will cut right through most socks, booties, and pants; tights and dresses don't stand a chance. Look for warm fabrics like flannel, corduroy, and velour, and long sleeves and legs. Provide complete protection, even on short car rides. Get a warm suit with good insulation to fit in car seats, strollers, backpacks, and carriers. To cut that initial chill when the car seat's been freezing along with the car, a small quilt or thick blanket, a crocheted throw, or a wool car seat cover will warm up much faster than the thin pad the manufacturer provides. (Think how much your baby would like a seat cover that's been in the house overnight!)

Loss of heat in a newborn can easily become loss of weight, so a soft, pull-on cap is essential in any season. Babies have big heads, and not very much hair; there's a lot of surface area that can lose heat. The temperature in homes and hospitals doesn't begin to compare with the uterine environment newborns are used to!

Older babies need protection, too. Those nippy winter winds can make little ears ache and babies cry. Cover them completely with knitted or fleece caps with ear flaps that tie under the chin, or better yet, ear and neck flaps with buttons or Velcro.

The ultimate protection for your baby is your own body heat. With your baby in a carrier or sling close to your body and a coat or warm poncho over both of you, you can be assured that while you are outdoors, your baby is comfortably cozy. ♥

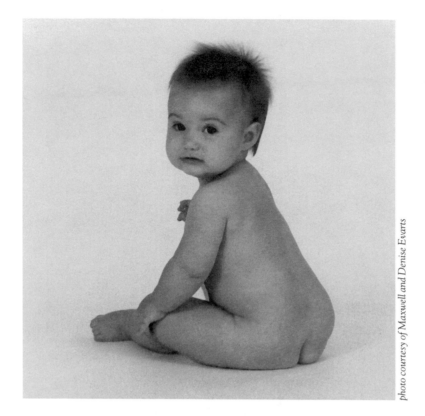

photo courtesy of Maxwell and Denise Evarts

Diapering

Diapers go with babies; there's no arguing that. We all have to deal with them, but systems and supplies vary considerably. In this chapter our contributors discuss their experiences, including the environmental impacts and the economics of diapering. Our readers chime in with their diaper discourse.

In the grand scheme of things, our individual diapering choices don't have an enormous impact on life or the planet; there are trade-offs any way you go. But as with most things, if we educate ourselves about the options, we can at least feel good about the path we choose. After all, if each of us is going to change a diaper 5,000 or more times for each of our children, we ought to feel good about the way we do it.

Motherwear photo

A Whirlwind Tour of Diapering

BY ZIPORAH HILDEBRANDT

I know how overwhelming a new baby and all his needs can be, especially for first-time parents. You're learning how to be responsible for a tiny, helpless being who seems to communicate with you primarily by crying. It's hard, without experience, to make the best choices you can for your baby's health and comfort, your own convenience and peace of mind, and your budget.

There is no simple answer to the question "What kind of diaper should I use?" I believe cotton diapers are better for your baby, your budget, and the environment. However, no single diaper or system is going to work at all times for everyone. The key to diapering, as with so many other aspects of parenting, is to do what works for you.

There are basics about diapering that apply in most cases. First—the changing area. This is where you keep everything you need for a diaper change, and I do mean everything! You'll spend a lot of time here in the first year, so pick a place that's pleasant and convenient. When choosing a location, consider where you spend the most time. If you have a large house or don't like stairs, you might want more than one changing area.

Start with a changing table or an ordinary table or dresser. Place a foam pad, a soft, thick quilt, or a big folded towel on top. Large, rubberized flannel cloths are comfortable and handy for protecting what's underneath, and a clean, rectangular diaper right on the changing surface makes it easy to clean up without having to wash everything frequently.

There should be space for clean diapers and covers, a roll of toilet tissue, a bowl or squeeze bottle of water, small washcloths or wipes, and a wastebasket. You'll also want diaper clips or pins, if you use them, natural creams or ointments, corn starch (not talcum powder; it can be harmful if inhaled), and a couple of toys to entertain your baby. If you keep the diaper pail in another room, you'll need a spot at the changing area to put used diapers and wipes where your baby can't touch them with hands or feet.

Be very sure everything you need is right there, as you must keep one hand on your baby *at all times*. As babies get older, stronger, and more mobile, diaper changes can be boring for them and a trial for the unprepared adult.

After you lay your baby down and take off the used diaper, clean his skin thoroughly, getting among all the folds and creases to be sure nothing is left behind. Remove clothes that have gotten wet or soiled; for this it is helpful to have clean clothes nearby. For really messy clean-ups, just pop your baby (not an infant) under the tub faucet with the drain open. (Feel the water first.) It's quick, it's easy, and most babies love being in the water. Air dry, or pat with a soft cloth before putting on another diaper. This is the only time your baby's skin really gets to breathe! Put on a new diaper snugly, and cover it well to avoid leaks.

Some toddlers require an entirely different technique. Forget the changing table—get used to diapering on the go. The suits with snaps all the way down the legs are great at this age. By raising the bottom snap of one leg over your toddler's shoulder to meet the bottom snap of the other leg, you can give yourself plenty of room to get that clean diaper on. Soon you'll get used to following your active child around on your knees! Many toddlers delight in taking off their diapers. Try turning the covers around so the Velcro is in the back.

Then there's the bed. Whether you have a crib or a family bed, you'll want to be prepared for midnight leaks. Though babies, even newborns, urinate less frequently while asleep, crying babies, sodden sheets, and dripping diapers still happen—and are no fun at 3 AM. Do you reach for a super-absorbent disposable? They do hold an incredible amount of fluid, but there are serious questions concerning the safety of these products, especially when in prolonged contact with skin. With forethought and the currently available array of innovative diapers, your baby should be able to feel comfortable all night.

You'll need two diapers. Position one diaper in the usual way, and fit another inside it to add layers in the middle. Make sure the part of the diaper that will be under the sleeping baby gets the most layers. (But keep comfort in mind, too; you don't want your baby's hips to be four inches higher than his chest!) Purchase a larger size cover to accommodate the added bulk of double-diapering. Avoid leaks by making sure none of the diaper sticks out of the cover! The chill of a leak can awaken a baby sooner than the discomfort of wetness.

Even with these measures, there will be times you'll have to change a diaper when you're half asleep. Make sure you have everything you'll need close at hand. Set up a fresh double diaper and cover right by the bed. Pick a spot to dispose of the wet diaper. Get a damp washcloth (or whatever you choose) and a dry cloth to wipe—any dampness, not just urine, can irritate sensitive skin.

Leak-proof the bed. Wherever your baby sleeps, place some kind of waterproof layer under the mattress pad to protect the mattress. A variety of products are available, and even a plastic trash bag under a towel and a bottom sheet will do fine. If your baby sleeps in your bed, consider placing her on a wool blanket or pad. The pad will absorb any leaks while remaining warm and keeping her warm, too.

If your sheet is damp, you might try putting a large towel down over the damp part. Since you have a protective layer over your mattress, a little dampness isn't cause for worry. Change the sheet in the morning.

Your baby doesn't soak a diaper and wake up at night in order to drive you crazy—really. The time will come when she sleeps through the night, wet or not. Before too long, she'll sleep through the night dry. But some kids, especially those prone to allergies, may wet the bed long after they're out of diapers during the day. It all happens at a child's own pace. Just accept it and go with the flow, so to speak. Diapers are just a part of having a baby in the house. ♥

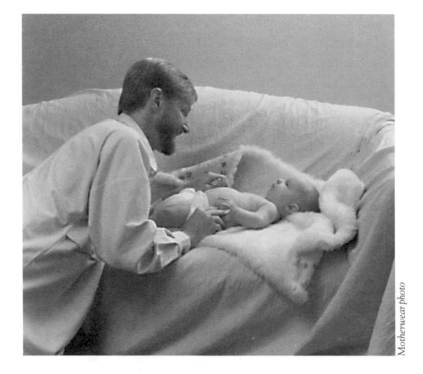

Motherwear photo

Cotton Diapers: Better for Baby, Better for the World

BY DAYNA HAMP

At the tender age of thirteen, I had the pleasure of helping my sister care for her baby. Each day that I baby-sat, I faithfully washed a load of diapers, carefully measuring the bleach and detergent, as the diapers had to be disinfected and dinge-free to pass my mother's and sister's scrupulous standards. I don't remember diaper rashes or infections or finding the diapers an inconvenience in any way. Instead, those diapers provided fond memories, as folding time became a game to see who could pop them the loudest and fold them the fastest. To this day I love the smell and feel of freshly washed and folded diapers.

Years later, when my first baby arrived, I had my own choices to make about diapers. Would I follow my family's tradition of cloth diapers, or would I choose the new "super-dry" disposables? Lovingly, my mother supplied me with dozens of new cloth diapers and reminded me of those time-honored washing instructions. I used them faithfully—when it was convenient. When it wasn't, I headed to the store for a box of disposables.

Had I known then what I do now, I would have stuck with good old cotton. Imagine going from a soft, cool, breathable diaper to a stiff, sticky, paper and plastic one. Try the "touch test," then ask yourself which you would rather wear twenty-four hours a day.

I was attracted at first to those "super absorbent, leak-free" disposables. Like so many parents, I put them on and left them on, because I couldn't tell my baby was wet until he was soaked. This led to some major diaper rashes. I have since learned that disposable diaper manufacturers use chemical polymer crystals to mask wetness. These crystals (the same that can cause toxic-shock-syndrome for tampon users) absorb up to one hundred times their weight in liquid, turning it into gel. Not only is this an outrageous amount of urine for a baby or toddler to tote around, but those thirsty little crystals, when not absorbing urine, are taking much-needed moisture from babies' delicate skin.

I wasn't too worried about chemicals until I learned that most of the chemicals in disposables have not been tested for their long-term effects. There is now concern about the migration of these chemicals to reproductive organs. One hospital noticed an outbreak of severe bleeding and oozing diaper rash in newborns and quickly discontinued the use of the culprit—a name-brand disposable diaper. It was noted during an investigation that employees in the diaper factories were also having reactions to the chemical. Time-tested cotton diapers pose no such threat to their innocent young users.

Diaper rash may signal an allergy to food or to a new laundry detergent. If you are nursing, it might mean "lay off the chocolate" or "no more hot sauce." A rash might also occur when a baby is teething, as the urine becomes more alkaline during this time. With cloth diapers, I am able, through process of elimination, to identify and solve the problem. With disposables, however, I experienced a whole new set of problems. My baby was constantly exposed to perfumes, bleaching agents, and chemicals. In addition, the elasticized leg openings and plastic outer barrier (designed to keep mom and dad drier) made it impossible to tell if my baby was having a food reaction or a chemical one.

The fact that disposables, with their impermeable plastic barrier, cannot "breathe" increases the risk of over-hydration and can raise a baby's skin tempera-ture to dangerous levels. Not only can this cause severe heat rash, but when the heat combines with wetness on or near the skin during the bacterial breakdown of urine, the risk of infection is greatly increased. This is why experts are now recommending breathable diaper covers, such as wool or cotton, rather than plastic, rubber, or nylon.

In contrast, porous cotton diapers quickly absorb wetness while allowing fresh air to circulate to the skin. This "breathability" permits evaporation of wetness as well as ammonia, a by-product of the bacterial breakdown of urine. These qualities account for cotton's long history as first-aid for open wounds.

I once thought that diaper rash was an unavoidable part of diapering, even though it usually landed us in the doctor's office. In actuality, diaper rash is largely a twentieth-century complication brought on by our modern diapering methods. Disposable wearers are three to five times more likely than cloth wearers to have a diaper rash and are ten times more likely to suffer severe rashes and infections.

Disposable diaper manufacturers refute the rash argument, stating that rashes occur when parents don't change diapers frequently enough. These same manufacturers tell us that babies in disposables stay dry longer because "when they're wet, they're dry," so parents leave the diaper on because it doesn't *feel* wet.

A U.S. Consumer Product Safety Commission report stated that babies have died from suffocation and asphyxiation due to unusual contact with the stuffing, outer plastic lining, and tabs of disposable diapers. Tabs have also been known to tear skin. This report includes complaints about rashes, allergic reactions, and injury from foreign objects such as wood splinters, found in the diapers themselves. Needless to say, cloth diapers pose none of these hazards. Parents concerned about sticking the baby with pins should try pinless covers or diaper clips.

Then there's the "disposable" issue itself. In this country alone, we throw over eighteen billion disposable diapers annually into our quickly disappearing landfills. That's 4,275,000 tons of hazardous waste *every year* that will remain for the next five centuries, because disposables, regardless of the claims, are not biodegradable. Almost one third of our landfills are in the process of being closed, and few new ones are scheduled to open, due to tighter regulations, rising costs, and more resistance from communities.

Every child who is diapered in cloth will reduce by one ton the annual load on the waste stream. That means you and I can make a significant difference in today's increasing refuse problem.

Another problem arises because rinsing the tremendously absorbent disposable diapers results in a very wet, very heavy diaper. Instead of being emptied and rinsed, the diapers are trashed, piling more than eighty million pounds of fecal matter into landfills each year. More than one hundred viruses have been found surviving in trashed disposables. Since babies can pass viruses (live vaccines from routine immunizations remain alive for several weeks), this presents a real health hazard. Not only does this needlessly expose sanitation workers to disease, but these same viruses can leach into the ground, polluting underground water supplies. Airborne viruses carried by flies and other insects make the situation even worse.

Annually, the manufacturing of disposable diapers wastes nearly one hundred thousand tons of plastic and an average of one million tons of wood pulp in the United States alone. That means we are destroying approximately 250,000 trees every year to make single-use diapers. On the contrary, cotton diapers are durable, washable, and reusable, and you will probably find new uses for them after your diapering years are over. (We use them for dusting and cleaning until they are virtually threadbare.)

After considering the facts, I decided that conscientious diapering, like conscientious living, means doing what is right instead of what is most convenient. It's certainly an argument worth its weight in cotton. ♥

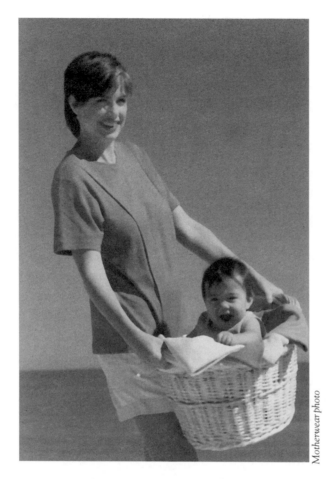

Motherwear photo

Mothers Share: Our readers discuss
Diaper Laundering

COMPILED BY JODY WRIGHT

"If I am doing something wrong, let me know!" one mother commented after telling us how she washed diapers. Of course the right way to launder diapers is any way that eliminates harmful bacteria and prevents diaper rash. The method will vary according to your facilities and circumstances, how old your baby is, and what is important to you.

I was amazed by the number of responses we got to this question. One of my favorites was this one: "My first, a daughter, was born while we were missionaries in a remote town in Bolivia, South America. I had to wash diapers every day by hand with water drawn from a cistern and heated on a stove. When it rained I had to hang them inside our one-room adobe house to dry. They dried like cardboard, and I had to iron them to soften them. When people tell me it's too much work to wash their own diapers, I tell them it is easier with an automatic washing machine and a dryer than hand-washing them outdoors when it is cold or raining."

What's involved in diaper handling? Pre-washing or soaking, detergents and soaps, washing rinsing, drying, folding, and storing them. Each can be handled differently, and you will need to put together a process that works well for you.

Mothers Share asked: How do you launder your diapers?

"I put dirty diapers into a lidded diaper bucket with no water in it. After a day or two, I place them in the washer and run a cold-water rinse cycle. (I figure this uses less water than flushing for each diaper plus filling the bucket, and it's sure easier). Then I wash them in hot water with about two-thirds to three-quarters of a cup of bleach for large load. I run a second rinse, and machine dry."

"I have a big pail that I fill with water, a half cup of Borax and a half cup of white vinegar to inhibit the odor and the growth of bacteria. Every other day I dump the contents of the pail into the washer and run a rinse, followed by a complete hot-water cycle. After one more rinse, they go into the dryer. I only use chlorine if my baby has had diarrhea. I use Ivory soap—no detergent. The diaper covers go right in with the diapers and hang dry. Cotton diapers are great for the environment, and washing them myself gives me control over what chemicals are put in the diapers. Although they may have some stains, imagine what a diaper service must use to get them sparkling white!"

"We wash diapers ourselves, as there is no diapering service. We wash in a machine with hot water every three days. We use Dreft to wash, one hot water rinse, dry on a clothesline."

"We use a tissue to scrape instead of flushing. Then the diapers go into a pail dry, then right into the machine. We rinse and spin, then wash normally. Saves time and water."

"Since I wash every day, I don't always soak diapers. I just throw them in a bucket (with lid)."

"I wash two times per week. Rinse diapers in toilet once a day. Wring out and put in pail. On wash day, I soak them in a utility tub with Borax for up to six hours, then spin out the water in my washer. Wash with Dreft or Ivory Snow in hot water/cold rinse cycle. Dry without Bounce sheets in dryer."

"I live in southeast Alaska with no electricity or running water. Our water is collected off roofs into garbage cans. It is heated by reservoir on a wood cook stove. Soiled diapers are put to soak in a five-gallon bucket with water. Wet-only diapers go into another bucket with no water in it. The buckets either go to a laundromat seven miles away or are washed in an old wringer washer run by our generator. I rinse soiled diapers by hand all at once in their bucket, or sometimes just dump the whole mess in a machine at the laundromat, with no rinse. Diaper covers, the same. Wash two times per week. I use Ivory Snow, no rinses, soaks, etc. My three-month-old only gets rashes when I use disposables, it seems, so I don't use them at all anymore."

"I have three dozen diapers and wash them once a week. (My daughter is eight months old; when she was younger I had to wash them more frequently.) I have two diaper pails (a full large one was too heavy) which I fill with water mixed with a little Ivory Snow or Dreft detergent. On wash day, I set the washer on 'rinse and spin' with the temperature on warm. (Hot at this point sometimes causes staining.) Then I do a normal cycle using Ivory Snow or Dreft and hot water."

"I wash about every three days in hot water using Ivory Snow detergent. I don't use a rinse in the pail, nor do I double-rinse them in my machine. I clean the pail out with soap and hot water."

"I wash diapers by hand when wet or soiled, then rinse and wash with baby's clothes."

"I wash them in biodegradable detergent and occasionally use bleach to whiten and sterilize them. Hot wash, cold rinse. The first rinse, I add one cup of vinegar to help remove soap, and then I give them one more clear rinse."

"My daughter has very sensitive skin and gets rashes very easily—even from Calendula Baby Soap! I use a diaper service now, but before we moved to this town, I had to wash them myself. I added a half cup of chlorine bleach to the hot wash, and then rinsed twice, or until I couldn't smell the bleach anymore. In the last rinse, I added some vinegar. I found that any detergent or soap I used wouldn't rinse out enough for my daughter, so I ended up using Shaklee Basic H and Borax in the wash. The Basic H really got out the stains, to my surprise. Basic H works very well on the covers, too, both wool and cotton. I usually wash them by hand quickly in the sink, hang dry, and every few days put them in with the family laundry."

"Most days are sunny here so I dry them in the sun. When my daughter seems to have trouble with rashes, and I know it isn't because she'd been left in a wet diaper too long, I add a half cup vinegar to the rinse of each load. Between the sun (UV light to kill the germs and bacteria) and the vinegar (to neutralize the urea), we haven't had any other problems. I would guess that washing our own diapers requires maybe one to two hours of extra work a week." ♥

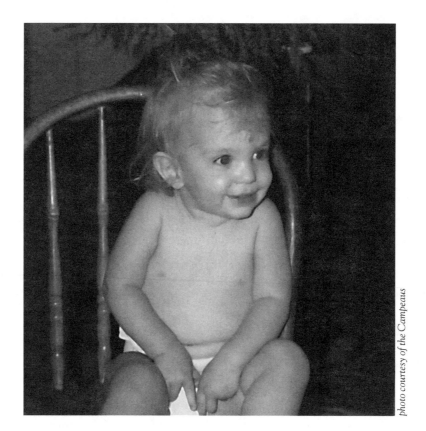

photo courtesy of the Campeaus

Diapers: Comfort, Convenience, and Health

BY ZIPORAH HILDEBRANDT

Children are in diapers up to twenty-four hours a day for two to four years. The first thing to remember about healthy, comfortable diapering is to change the diaper promptly when it's wet or soiled. Newborns need twelve to fifteen changes every day. Their skin is particularly sensitive and vulnerable to irritation from prolonged contact with moisture. And there is a type of bacteria that converts elements of the urine into ammonia, which is extremely irritating.

Since a baby is covered by a diaper most of the time, there is limited air circulation to the skin in this area. Wearing a diaper raises the temperature of a baby's skin. Any kind of cover on the diaper will cut down on air circulation and raise the temperature even more. This increased warmth creates a happy habitat for rash-causing bacteria, so the secret is prompt changing and plenty of air.

Cotton breathes. Cotton diapers, even when wet, permit air on a baby's skin. Urine will soak through cotton, however, so for the protection of our homes, cars, and clothing, we cover diapers with something waterproof to prevent leaks. Cotton, wool, and nylon diaper covers are waterproof, yet still breathe. Rubber, vinyl, and plastic covers are, like the plastic in disposable diapers, impervious to moisture— and air. For this reason alone, your baby will be more comfortable in cotton diapers with breathable covers. If your baby is prone to rashes, it's even more important to use the most breathable covers you can find.

Some babies are hyper-sensitive to fragrances and other chemicals in soaps, detergents, wipes, lotions, and disposable diapers. If your baby shows signs of sensitivity, discontinue the use of the suspected product. Try other brands, and experiment with different systems until you find one your baby tolerates. Many wipes contain alcohol and chemicals that can irritate skin. Try a "natural" brand, soap and water, or just water. Change soiled diapers immediately so fecal matter doesn't crust on your baby's skin.

As for comfort, how many adults wear plastic? Given a choice, do you think babies would choose soft, breathable cotton, or perfumed, crinkly plastic and paper? Try it: rub a disposable against your cheek, then a cotton diaper. Which feels better? Which cotton diapers are softest? In my experience, flannel diapers are consistently softest. Pre-folds I washed myself were the harshest, while pre-folds from a diaper service were in the middle, neck and neck with gauze diapers from a department store. When we moved to an area with softer water, the diapers I washed myself were even softer than those from the diaper service. It all depends on your water and washing technique and what your diaper service has available. Diaper services typically buy softer, higher quality diapers that are not available in stores.

There is particular reason for concern over the hazards of super-absorbent disposable diapers. These products contain a chemical that can cause severe skin infections and has been associated with toxic shock syndrome. This chemical, when linked with polymers, gives diapers their amazing ability to absorb and hold fluids. Once the skin becomes wet, it too is subject to the absorptive powers of the diaper. Incredible as it may seem, the absorbency is so potent, it can actually draw out the fluid between the skin's cells, causing shriveling of the skin.

The whole diapering issue is worth your careful consideration. Though they may seem interminable while you're in them, the diaper years are over soon. It's worth your child's health to choose wisely. ♥

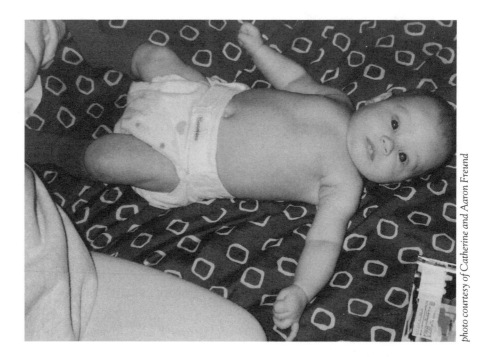

photo courtesy of Catherine and Aaron Freund

What to Do About Diaper Rash

BY ZIPORAH HILDEBRANDT

In the 1940s, diaper rash was almost unheard of in one-month-old infants. More recently, a study in the *Journal of Pediatrics* found that 54% of one-month-old infants in disposable diapers had rashes, and 16% had severe rashes. Of those diapered in cloth, only 18% had rashes, and none had severe rashes.

Fifty years ago, plastic hardly existed. Most people used "soakers" or wool or rubber pants to prevent diapers from leaking. Wool soakers were often knit at home and boiled to draw the knit closer together. Like the wool covers of today, they were very breathable.

Why do more babies have rashes now than then? Why do so many more infants develop a rash with disposables? It could be that disposables aren't changed as frequently as cloth diapers, because they feel dry. Allergic reactions to the chemicals and perfumes in disposables probably contribute. Another culprit is the plastic liners in disposables, which raise a baby's skin temperature and cut off air circulation.

Plastic, non-porous diaper covers can raise a baby's skin temperature to 104 ° F. The warm, moist environment, combined with urine and feces, is a perfect breeding ground for bacteria. Disposables feel dry because of the chemicals in them.

But the urine and feces are still there in the "dry" diaper, long after it should have been changed. If a baby's skin is already broken, irritated, and vulnerable, there could be infection.

Diaper rash commonly appears as areas of rough, red skin, or patches of small red pimples. Whiteheads are a sign of mild infection. Raw spots indicate a more serious condition. A rash that appears beyond the diaper area is likely to be a sign of an allergic reaction, unless it is obviously an infection that has spread from diaper rash.

Most diaper rash can be prevented with the following measures: Change diapers as soon as they are wet or soiled. Use cotton diapers with breathable wool or cotton covers. Let your baby's bottom dry out a few hours each day. Wash the diaper area well between changes, and be sure to wipe off all soap residue. If you are washing your own diapers, be sure the soap or detergent is completely rinsed. Add a half cup of vinegar to the final rinse to balance the pH and as a fabric softener. Hang them to dry in the sunshine; it's a potent sterilizer! Do not use fabric softeners in your dryer. If your baby gets a rash from diaper service diapers, call them, change services, or switch to washing at home.

If there is a persistent rash accompanied by an ammonia smell in the wet diaper or bedding, you may need to resort to stronger methods of sterilization. An ammonia smell is caused by a bacteria that is not easily killed by soap or detergent. Add chlorine bleach to the wash according to manufacturer's directions. Boiling diapers is quite effective. Add one half to one cup of vinegar to the final rinse. Hang bedding, covers, and clothing in the sun.

Diaper services thoroughly sterilize their diapers. If your baby has a persistent rash, let the diaper service know. A rash may be an allergy to soap, wipes, detergent or other chemical residues, or possibly to food or an environmental influence such as dust or perfume. Experiment with different brands. Use the preventive tips above.

If the rash appears as rough, red areas, a healing ointment can be helpful. An herbal ointment or oil containing calendula, aloe vera, and vitamin E is soothing and healing. Vegetable oil, zinc oxide ointment, vegelatum, A&D ointment, and lanolin can help. Avoid steroids, powders, hormones, products containing mineral oil, and lotions with fragrance, alcohol or preservatives.

If the rash is in the form of pimples, air and sun are the best healers. Let your baby go diaperless whenever possible. Infants can be laid on the floor on top of a couple of diapers, and the diapers replaced as needed. Babies love to be naked: just be sure the room is warm enough for them. Up to six months of age, babies prefer room temperatures in the low 80s. (And keep in mind, the air is colder on the floor.) ♥

photo courtesy of Susan Love

Lifestyles

Before the experimental period of the sixties, society was not very accepting of people who chose to deviate from the norm. The radical behaviors of that decade seem to have legitimized the variety of personal choices that evolved into today's lifestyles. Breastfeeding is not the norm, but what a relief it is that this most natural of nurturing behaviors is no longer scorned.

That's what lifestyle is all about—the choices we make about how we live, where we go, how we raise our children, and what we eat, wear, and do. Offered here are perspectives on a variety of lifestyle issues and choices. There may be some options here you didn't know you had, choices you never thought of making.

The choices we make as parents have a lifelong impact on our children. They affect our quality of life, our communities, and our planet. We all want to make the best choices, but everyone's "best" will be different. What's important is that you listen to your heart and do what works best for you and your family.

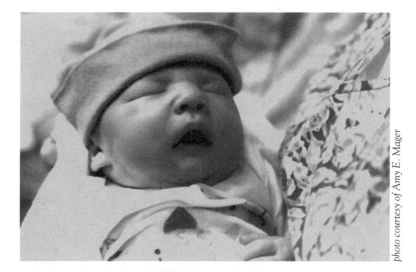

photo courtesy of Amy E. Mager

Home Birth

BY SHERYL STETTES KRAMER

Home birth has intrigued me for as long as I can remember. Birth seems such a natural part of life. I marvel that for centuries upon centuries, women have given birth and the propagation of the human family continues. In times past, there existed only limited medical care and intervention, yet still we humans have multiplied. Birth must be something women could do on their own or this would not be so.

When I joined the number of expectant parents, I visited an obstetrician. He informed me that I should expect a C-section. What was his reason? I was high-risk. Why? I had never had a baby before.

Surgery was not what I had in mind when I had hoped to conceive and bear a child. Disturbed at this news, I saw a small advertisement for a support group designed for women who either had had cesareans in the past and were hoping to avoid them in the future, or were hoping to avoid a cesarean on their first birth. I went. There were about thirty women present. Several spoke, each sharing her individual experience. What I heard that night startled me into reality. I heard women explain how they labored in the hospital, the physician pronounced "failure to progress" and a C-section was ordered, only to find out the next morning their OB had left on a previously scheduled vacation. I heard another story of a woman who was told her baby would be much too large for her to deliver. She had a C-section and the baby was born three pounds smaller than the physician had estimated. I heard stories of women manipulated by their doctors for the sake of convenience.

Could it be this was happening to me?

Following the logic my physician used would mean that every first-time mother would be labeled high-risk. My suspicion grew as I realized my calculated due date was late in December. I wondered if he just didn't want to miss the turkey and trimmings to deliver my baby. I certainly didn't believe lack of childbirth experience made me high-risk. There were no other complications.

I shopped for a doctor who did not share his view and found one who had a four-percent C-section rate. I had an uneventful pregnancy and delivered a 7 lb. 10 oz. girl without the intervention of drugs.

Two years later, I found myself expecting and in another city. I asked around to see if there were any doctors who would deliver a baby in a hospital without drugs, IVs, internal fetal monitoring, a shave, an enema, and lots of restrictions on laboring and birthing positions. I could find none. I just wanted to have a baby the old-fashioned way and let nature take its course. Unfortunately, no hospital in the area allowed that kind of arrangement. And no doctor was willing to put himself on the line and disregard hospital policy. The city has a number of hospitals offering birthing rooms, but while they have moved their technology into a room with blue walls and flowered bedspreads, their attitude is still the same. The prevailing thinking seems to be that women need their children extracted from them and that birth is a dangerous time in a woman's life that requires continual monitoring and intervention.

Someone gave me the phone number of a certified midwife who did home deliveries. I telephoned her and we had an interview. She agreed to deliver the baby. She was a registered nurse who had also completed midwifery training. She did all of my prenatal checkups and paid such close attention to my health that it put any physician who had ever cared for me to shame. We talked a lot about the birth. We mapped out where it would take place. We discussed how I would cope with the pain. We decided who would be present.

When labor began, she came to my home and coached me. I was allowed to move freely and assume whatever position was most comfortable. I was relaxed because I was in my own home, which made things more comfortable. The labor progressed rapidly. She, together with my husband, delivered my son weighing 8 lb. 6 oz. After a brief rest, she helped me into an herbal bath in my own bathtub. My baby and I napped in my own bed.

There is something that feels satisfying about birthing in that environment. Medication, intervention, and a clinical setting that disallows natural birthing positions alters the reality of the birth experience. We can do it. ♥

photo courtesy of Lise Alexander of Beginnings

Choreographing a Family

BY JODY WRIGHT

Some days I feel great about my parenting. Other days, we forget the dental appointment, one of the children comes down with the flu, I'm unprepared for an important meeting at work, and everyone gets to school late.

I've learned not to feel bad about my parenting on the bad days; I blame it on poor choreography.

On stage, choreography is the design of a dance: defining what move comes when and where they take the dancer. Each person has to be in synchronicity with the others. In family choreography, we're home or in the car when it's time for the baby's nap, there's a snack in the bag when we pick up a child after school, there's plenty of gas in the car when we have to get a child to the orthodontist, the field trip permission slip is signed and returned on time, and amidst it all we have left time to get our own needs met. Whether you are employed outside the home or have full-time child-care responsibilities, choreography is what can dictate how you feel about your day, and ultimately how you feel about your family.

Essentially, family choreography is planning: looking at the week, day, or moment and solving each of the problems that are posed by it. I've found a number of things to help me with this. Most obvious, of course, is a good calendar. If you want to share responsibilities with a partner, your family calendar needs to be in a common place—posted on the refrigerator for example. It needs to have enough room to record all of the unusual activities of the day, with locations, times, etc. A nearby bulletin board for posting notes (appointment cards, directions, schedules, etc.) is helpful, too. Check it daily and look ahead to see what is coming up. Find a time at the beginning of each week to discuss the schedule with everyone involved. At this point you can assign responsibilities for finding sitters, leaving work early, having dinner ready, etc.

The state of your house and the organization you bring to the physical things in your life are also important in the art of family choreography. Remembering a dental appointment for a child won't get you there if you can't find the child's boots, toothbrush, and stuffed rabbit. Watch for recurring problems and find solutions to them: a shelf for shoes by the front door, a supply of extra toothbrushes, a special chair for the rabbit when it's not being toted around.

Rhythms and habits are the day-by-day ways we choreograph our lives without thinking about every detail. A morning schedule that works, thinking about the next night's dinner as you clean up the night before, a weekly schedule of who picks up whom—all these things free you from starting from scratch every day. Look at the regular events in your life, and make sure those things are in order and clear to all involved.

Communication and clarity are of utmost importance. If you thought your partner was going to pick up your son at noon and he thought *you* were, it's not going to be a good day. Put things in writing, repeat the plan on your way out the door, and let others involved know what the plan is. Avoid making assumptions. Make a phone call if you suspect that things aren't clear.

There is another area that choreography concerns: safety. Many accidents, especially around cars, are the result of poor choreography. Let your children know *exactly* what you need from them. As you park the car, you might say, "I need you to stay in your seat while I get the bags out of the trunk and put the baby in the carrier. Then I'll open the door for you." As you walk through traffic, give clear instructions. "Let's look both ways and then hold hands as we cross the street. Do you hear that car starting up? We have to watch out here for moving cars." By planning ahead and figuring out the safest way to do things, we not only choreograph the moment more safely, we train our children how to take care of themselves when we aren't there.

Even our moods can be affected by good planning. Difficulties can be averted at the hardest times of the day—late afternoon, before dinner, before bed—by making sure everyone has had a healthy snack, something to entertain themselves with, and an idea of what "the plan" is. Before bed at night I often make a checklist of everything that has to be done the following day. The next day I get as many things as possible accomplished by one in the afternoon, which allows me to get some control over my evenings and cope with an otherwise stressful time of day.

One last thing is important in family choreography: knowing that what is good for you is good for me, and vice versa. Trying to provide the best for everyone is hard work. Sometimes things degenerate into a quibble between my husband and me over who is sacrificing most. This is clearly the time to do some talking and find out what each of our own needs are, then bring the children's needs into focus. Part of being a family is supporting and sacrificing for one another, with the assumption that others will support and sacrifice also. (Don't expect that all will be equal; you'll only end up disappointed.) It is important to have a sense of fairness and balance. For the family to do well as a whole, *each* family member has to grow and be happy. ♥

photo courtesy of Gabrielle Shatan

Practical Tips
for the First Two Years

COMPILED BY ZIPORAH HILDEBRANDT

There are lots of books around telling parents what to do and what not to do. They're written by "the experts." What have real parents done? What, in retrospect, has seemed most useful? I asked some of the experts I respect most: other moms. This is what they said:

Take the time to childproof your house (install safety gates, insert outlet covers, remove choking and suffocating hazards, eliminate things to climb high on, cushion floors, etc.). Making the rooms you spend the most time in safe frees your precious time and energy to do housework, talk on the phone, read, or spend time with other family members. It's never safe to leave a child unattended, but you can make your "attending" much easier. And it's healthier for your baby to explore in a relaxed way, rather than in an atmosphere of uncertainty that the object of her current fascination could be suddenly removed.

Structure your time to include a variety of activities for both of you. Nobody likes a dull routine. Visit playgrounds, malls, friends, age-appropriate museums, exhibits, zoos, and libraries. Find other parents with same-age children to combine adventures. Time with other kids is an opportunity to work on social skills. You'll both enjoy the chance to relate with someone on your own level. Include time alone for yourself, too. Don't feel guilty—daily time alone will refresh you so your time together is even better.

Consider lowering your standards of neatness: Don't fold the laundry, live with a little mess here and there, etc. Prioritize so there's time and energy for the really important things: your baby, your partner, yourself.

Make sure you get enough exercise. If you need to purchase special equipment (a jogging stroller, nursing leotard, bike seat, or baby carrier) do it! The benefits of health, energy, enjoyment, and knowing you're doing something for yourself are well worth the investment. You'll be setting a good example for your children, too.

Spend time with nature. Humans evolved on the plains and woodlands, and contact with this most natural environment, be it only the grass at the park or the sand at the beach, is an important stimulus for your baby and a welcome recharge for you.

Don't forget vacations! You and your partner need a change of scenery, too. Don't just visit relatives—plan for a baby-friendly atmosphere where you'll have minimal responsibilities. They may not be like the vacations you used to have, but they will still be a pleasant break.

Spend time with your partner. It's easy to let the demands of parenting a baby consume your waking hours. Set aside time for just the two of you.

Talk with other parents you trust, especially when you're having a hard time. Many people have gone through the same frustrations and may have helpful suggestions. And it always helps to talk about how you're feeling.

Don't get hung up on every sniffle and sneeze. Invest in books on your child's health that empower you, rather than feed your paranoia. *How to Raise Healthy Children in Spite of Your Doctor*, *Homeopathy at Home*, and *Everybody's Guide to Homeopathic Medicine* will help you evaluate and treat minor health problems, saving you time, worry, and money, and your baby will benefit from ingesting fewer drugs. *Mothering* magazine is also an excellent source of health information.

Share the activities that are important to you with your baby, right from the beginning. Reading, dancing, singing, hiking, swimming, and games are all things she'll be doing with other children all too soon. You can prepare her at home for a smooth transition to her life outside the home. And you get all the fun of sharing with her now.

Model behaviors you want your child to copy: cleaning up messes, helping others, asking for help clearly and calmly, being polite, showing respect for others, being friendly, resolving conflicts, moderation with food, drink, and money, taking responsibility for your actions. Motherhood can bring out the best in you (as well as the worst!).

Read to your infants and toddlers. They enjoy the colorful pictures and the sound of your voice. It's a quiet, cuddling time for you both. Reading enhances language acquisition, increases attention span, improves patience, helps teach about people and the world, and stimulates the imagination. Make the children's room at the public library a regular destination. And there are more than books at libraries: You'll find toys, tapes, puzzles, games, special children's events (such as puppet shows and storytellers), and other parents and babies.

Don't be afraid to hold your baby as much as you want. There's no such thing as spoiling a baby; you can't hold her too much. Your baby wants you; listen to your heart.

Let go of images of the "perfect" child. He's himself, and not here to fit into your expectations. Let yourself grieve, if necessary, for the child you longed for, and love the child you have. He's with you for a reason.

Don't rush into the developmental stages. Trusting your child's biological wisdom is far superior to striving to fit in among the statistics.

Take photos and videos of these precious early months and years. Your baby will grow up very quickly. And don't forget to take just as many photos of second and third babies!

Most of all, enjoy and appreciate this truly brief time when your child is still small enough to hold in one arm and fall asleep nursing on your lap. It may seem like an eternity, but any month now your baby will be walking and talking. Suddenly he'll be more interested in his own activities than in you, and then school . . . . One day you'll realize the baby stage is gone forever, so appreciate him while he's here. ♥

My Four Miracles

BY JODY WRIGHT

When a baby is born to you, you know that he or she has somehow been chosen by God to be yours. Though three of our children came to us through adoption, each one has come with that same sense of destiny.

My experience in getting my four children has made me feel that each of them was loaned to me with God's special blessing. Let me tell you their stories.

Olisa

For me, 1979 and the first months of 1980 were very depressing. I had been trying to get pregnant for over a year, and nothing was happening. The whole world seemed populated by pregnant women, and every twenty-four days my period came again.

I had a gnawing feeling that there was a child out there for me. Pursuing adoption was my one light. During a pre-adoption meeting, my husband, Prakash, and I learned about searching independently for a child to adopt and explored the idea of having a multi-racial family.

We spent six months going through the humiliating process of fertility testing and the equally laborious task of proving to an adoption agency that we would make good parents. We started spreading the word that we wanted to adopt. One Filipino friend wrote about us to a pregnant friend of hers, but months passed and no word came. By spring I had sunk into a deeper depression, spending several weekends in tears. I felt that my child was out there and I couldn't get to her.

One day I dried my tears and said to myself, "If she really *is* out there, I better get ready for her." I made a list of all the things that I would have to prepare for a new baby. There were sixteen things on my list, and I told myself that if I did one of them every weekend, she would come to me when I was done. I counted out sixteen weeks to the end of July, then added a few just to be sure. I refinished a chest and began to collect hand-me-downs, diapers, information about adoptive nursing, and whatever else I thought we'd need.

One day in July, just as I was recovering from a uterine infection caused by infertility work, I got a call from my friend's pregnant friend. She wanted us to consider adopting her baby! The next weekend we drove five hours to visit this woman, whose African-Filipino baby was due in two weeks. Somehow I knew it would be born the next Sunday, on the full moon. She called Sunday—in labor—and invited us to come. We put our already-packed suitcases in the car—and the accelerator pedal didn't work! It was just like all the stories we'd heard people tell of laboring women unable to get to the hospital. Lucky for us, we got another car and were on our way in a matter of hours.

Olisa was born into the arms of an African midwife exactly sixteen weeks from the day I had made my list. Giving up her baby was tremendously difficult for her mother, but economical, political, and social forces made it impossible to keep her. Early in her pregnancy she had asked God what she should do with her baby, and the letter about us arrived in her mailbox. Now, passing Olisa among loving arms, we spent four days helping one another through the painful emotions this transition brought forth. I was able to sit for long hours with her in my lap and look into her beautiful little face—and breastfeed a child that was going to be mine.

I loved getting home with this new baby and showing her off to all my friends and family. It was a moment I had dreamed of for years!

Mahajoy

When Olisa was two years old, I had a feeling there was another baby, somewhere, for us. Again we started telling friends of our desire to find a child. Olisa's mother contacted us in the beginning of September and asked if she could mention us to a friend in the Philippines. One Sunday some time later, I felt so intensely that I should get ready for a new baby, I got out all of Olisa's baby clothes and washed and repaired them. The next day I got a call from Mahajoy's mom in the Philippines inviting me to come.

As with Olisa's mom, economics, race, social expectations, and politics played strong roles in forcing Mahajoy's mother to consider adoption. Unfortunately, she also suffered from a great deal of emotional turmoil. A mother giving up her baby often feels that the new mother has everything she doesn't: a caring partner, a home, money to support a child, and worst of all, her baby.

For more than seven months I lived in the Philippines with my two-year-old and an infant whose mother couldn't make up her mind whether we were the right family for her daughter. Meanwhile, I was breastfeeding Mahajoy but not able to give myself totally to her for fear I would lose her. Between caring for two children, keeping everything sterile in a third-world country, doing all our laundry by hand, and cooking without refrigeration, I lost 20 pounds and got a serious case of postnatal depression.

I knew inside that Mahajoy was supposed to be with me. I recognized that gnawing feeling from the previous adoption, but there was nothing to do but wait for it to work out. After much pain on everyone's part the adoption was complete, and I finally brought nine-month-old Mahajoy home.

Liina

Now that we had adopted two children, I felt ready to face the risk of surgery. I knew that as I tried again to get pregnant I would have two beautiful children to help me keep perspective through the hard times. We decided to go ahead.

At first we were told that there was about a one-in-five chance of getting pregnant with fallopian-tube surgery. After a preliminary look, the surgeon thought the chances were even smaller. We decided to go for it anyway, augmenting the procedure in every way we could think of to increase the odds. I spent several months eating nutritious foods and taking care of my health. I researched homeopathics to help me heal and reduce the internal scarring. As I waited on the operating table, I imagined that my spiritual teacher was the one who was doing the surgery. Then I spent five and a half hours having my fallopian tubes opened and fibrous scar tissue removed.

Within seven weeks I was pregnant! The surgeon was astounded. He told my midwife that he had thought there was a one-in-a-thousand chance of success, then took the file home to see what he had done right. It was a very fulfilling pregnancy, and the natural birth of our beautiful daughter Liina was what I had always hoped for.

Emily

When Liina was two, we began having unprotected intercourse again. Four years later, I still hadn't gotten pregnant, so when we found out about a potential adoption, we decided to pursue it. We completed a very quick home study (by now it was clear we were good parents), and were all ready for a special-needs baby that had been born three months premature. It wasn't to be—the mom wasn't ready for the adoption.

We met with our social worker on a Monday afternoon to begin looking for another baby. She told us that just that morning she'd been given the file of a biracial baby who was due that month. She also said we were the only family she currently had in her files for a biracial child and sent us home to think about it.

We knew what we wanted before we got to our car. That afternoon, we presented the idea to our kids. Everyone gave an excited "OKAY." Everyone but Liina.

"Why not?" I asked. "We really want another baby."

"I just don't want to."

I decided on the psychological approach. "What would make you change your mind?"

"Gum."

"Gum?" I asked incredulously.

"Yes. Ten pieces of gum."

"If I gave you ten pieces of gum, you'd feel okay about us getting another baby."

"Yes."

"It's a deal!" We got her ten pieces of gum and called back the agency to tell them yes.

Friday came. We hadn't heard anything. My spirits dropped, and I wondered if it had all been a mirage. I didn't know whether to unpack the boxes and start preparing for a baby or not. I called our social worker, who said, "I'll call you back in a few hours. Don't worry, it's looking good." We only had to wait an hour. "Your baby was born Wednesday night. You can pick her up at 10:00 Monday morning."

Is it a coincidence that we went to *that* agency for a home study? That Emily's mother's visit to the agency was perfectly aligned with our appointment to begin our search? Is it a coincidence that Olisa and Mahajoy and Liina had all found their way, along three completely different routes, into our home and into our hearts? Not at all. Each of these was a miracle, and each was God's will.

Thank you, God, for giving us these wonderful children to raise for you. ♥

Why Pets Matter

BY BETH HERSH

We went a long time not having pets in our family. With three young children, a home, a car, and a job to maintain, I figured I had about all I could deal with. I'd already had my pet-of-a-lifetime: a dog I'd raised and loved from puppyhood, who lived in devotion to me for eleven years. When she died, I believed I was finished with pets.

The children had never really paid much attention to Maggie, so I was not prepared for their response to her death. They mourned and cried, told all their friends, and wrote stories about her in school. Much later they were still talking about Maggie and how much they missed her. I slowly began to realize that Maggie had become a symbol for everything they were missing because of changes in their lives.

Animals are a magical cross between dolls and friends. Often a child's emotions are projected onto a pet, as if putting feelings out makes them easier to understand and cope with. I had a guinea pig when I was an adolescent. She followed my feet when I walked, came when I called her, sat up and squeaked when I asked her to. It was an awkward time in my life, and I believe she helped me through. She was the perfect ice-breaker when a new friend would visit. When we were alone, I told her all the untellable things about myself. I cried so much into her fur that I think she was perpetually salty.

My children now have a dog and a cat. I watch their different ways of relating to them. My eleven-year-old claims the lesson of responsibility. She gets up early every morning to take the dog, Minga, for a walk. I see signs of her learning a most important skill that she'll project to her new baby-sitting duties: to spot a need and know how to fill it. She's the first to notice when Minga is unbearably wiggly, and she'll take her out and run her. She cuddles her and invites her onto her bed whenever she makes the sad and lonely eyes that dogs make so well. I often see Sara filling an empty water bowl, and she's the first to notice when we run low on dog or cat food.

Her sister will play with the dog, too. She calls Minga to follow her around the house. She brushes her and talks to her. Minga, in turn, gives the gift of true companionship. She gives her whole self: heart, soul, and body. Dogs hold no judgment. They forgive totally. Their greatest delight is your attention.

My youngest is the hardest hit by struggles in the outside world. Her sensitivity to the unknowing cruelty of other children shows in her body sometimes when she comes home from school. Her shoulders are round, and her head is down. Then I see her reaching out her arms and drawing an animal close. She cannot pass the cat without scooping her and holding her close to her heart. An armful of warm, purring fur or a large, soft dog leaning into her, oozing love and kisses, is the best therapy for any hurting heart.

Pets can be a bother. They can cost more money than you ever imagined and take more of your time and energy than you believed you had to give. But in the end, the lessons they teach just by being here and loving us are worth everything we give them and more. ♥

photo courtesy of Tineke Dahl

The Visitor

BY ALLENA JAMES

I had just nestled myself into my favorite chair, cup of tea at my side, book in my hand, baby at my breast, when the doorbell rang. "Come in," I called softly. It was my sister-in-law, Karen. I invited her to come in and pour herself a cup of tea. She asked if she could use my crib, because her two-month-old was due for his nap. "Sure," I said. "We won't be using it."

I took a sip of tea and looked down at my sweet child. He was gazing at me with those big, dark eyes from the angle that only a nursing mother gets to see. I felt my milk let down like a spring suddenly bubbling from the earth, and his sucking changed to accommodate the flow of milk.

A few minutes after she put her baby in the crib, Karen was upstairs again to see why he was crying. She came back to get the diaper bag and find a soother for him to suck on, then ran upstairs again. Finally, she came downstairs and sat on the couch. "You know," she said, "it's a shame you never use that crib. It's really beautiful and it just sits there collecting dust."

"I find it easier to keep the baby with me."

"Wouldn't it be better if he got used to sleeping in his own bed? Then you wouldn't have to sit there all afternoon." As she said this, her baby was starting to fuss again, and she got up to go to him.

I sipped at my tea and leaned my head back. Jason was nursing in his sleep now, his warm body nestled against mine as if he were still a part of me. His little rosebud lips let go of my nipple, and his head fell away from my breast. I lifted him up so I could smell his sweet, milky fragrance.

Karen, back again from upstairs, commented, "I suppose he'd wake up if you laid him down?"

"He might."

"How can you possibly get anything done? Don't you need time for yourself?"

"I think your baby's crying again," I answered.

She sighed as she rolled herself off the couch once more. "I really think you'd be a lot happier if you'd put him down and get him used to his own bed," she said, heading upstairs. I put my feet up on the stool, laid my head back, closed my eyes, and thought about what a tough life I had, being tied down like this.♥

Mothers Share: Our readers discuss
Fathers at Home

COMPILED BY JODY WRIGHT

As fathers, brothers, uncles, and partners, men are essential ingredients in most families. Yet, so often our culture can make men feel limited in their nurturing roles and abilities, even to the point of not knowing how to nurture. When a new baby arrives, both mother and baby need a lot of nurturing and support. Mothers naturally turn to husbands and partners for everything from diapers to grocery shopping to back rubs. How women and men handle this shift in expectations can set the tone for the new family.

Mothers Share asked: "How involved is the man in your household with the baby's care and with household maintenance? Any suggestions for increasing men's involvement?"

"I wanted to take this rare opportunity to sing the praises of my husband. Beginning with my pregnancy, my husband was 100 percent supportive. From back rubs to doing the lugging of the laundry and groceries, he has always been willing to help.

"When our son was born, he had his hands full, running the house with a ten-year-old boy and a fifteen-year-old girl, keeping school schedules straight, and still finding time to spend rocking the baby so I could have time to myself. Bill has done everything from changing diapers, waking up at night with sick children, attending school concerts, and waiting up until 1 A.M. to drive our daughter home from a party. His example seems to be rubbing off on our son, who is very involved in his baby brother's life. Billy hasn't changed a diaper yet, but he plays with the baby and entertains him when he is fussy or cranky. Billy is always there to help with the baby and isn't ashamed to be doing it."

"My husband is more involved than one would normally expect, which stemmed from his ten-year desire to have a child. Fortunately he was interested in everything that concerned a baby—from preparing nipples to buying the right crib. My not buying the particular one that interested him was a major issue. So most of

photo courtesy of the Smith-Bovés

the time I let him have his way, to keep his interest alive. He made sure the baby had everything he needed and wanted.

"I suggest that mothers keep their husbands involved and not be domineering. Avoid the urge to tell him what to do, when to do it, and how it should be done, unless of course he asks. When he offers to dress the baby, forget about perfect color combinations. If it bothers you a lot, put the baby's clothes in stacks, so Dad can see exactly what you have in mind. Encourage him in every way to assist by asking him to hold the baby while you do something else. Slip away for a few minutes at a time and show that you trust his ability to care for your child. Tell him how much you appreciate his help."

"If you are with your baby all day, let go when Dad comes home. Generally men are more interested when they are made to feel a part of baby's life and care."

"After a long wait to have a baby, my husband is the delighted father of our fourteen-week-old girl. He is self-employed and is able to come home several times a day to visit, change diapers, and give me a break. He gets up to change the baby for *every* nighttime feeding and delivers her to me to nurse as I lie in the warm bed. I haven't had to bathe her since she was three weeks old! He is supporting us financially and does not have time for much housekeeping—but he's delighted to help care for the baby."

"I avoid correcting every detail of what my husband does around the house to help with the baby—he is just learning to do a lot of these things, and, like all of us, he needs encouragement and praise. I am learning to ask—a lot—rather than trying to do everything myself and be frustrated. He is willing to do a lot more than I'd ever guessed, with the new inspiration of our baby girl."

"My husband is a pretty involved father! I am blessed and thankful for it. However, there are times when I need his help and he isn't there. My tendency is to say nothing and deal with it on my own. The result is frazzled nerves and a bad attitude toward my husband."

"What I am excited to share is a communication tool we've just discovered. It's something I believe *every* couple could benefit from: *How to Talk so Your Mate Will Listen and Listen so Your Mate Will Talk*, a book by Nancy L. Van Pelt. We are reading it out loud together, taking notes on the practical suggestions, and practicing what she teaches! It is so important to learn to say exactly what we feel, to allow each other to have feelings without judging whether they are right or not, and to show that we care about each other's feelings. I am convinced that the vast majority of marriages could use improved communications. And I believe that the result of better verbal interaction is an increased desire to get involved and be helpful to one another. It is helping us. I hope others will do it, too. Love must be unconditional, and our commitment to it must be 100 percent." ♥

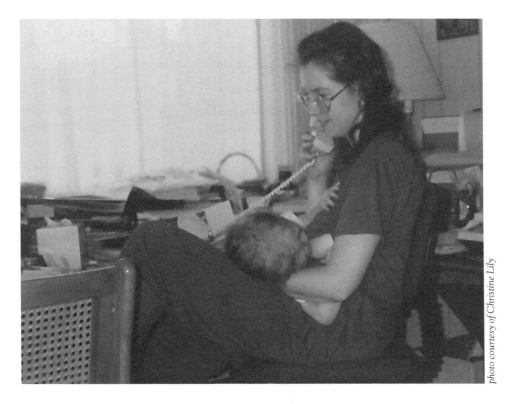

photo courtesy of Christine Lily

Is Working at Home for You?

BY JODY WRIGHT

In a recent *Parenting* magazine poll of parents with young children, 40 percent of the women and 36 percent of the men said that the best of all possible worlds would be to work at home for pay. Working at home can be a great experience, a big disappointment, or somewhere in between. If you've ever dreamed about working at home, here are some questions for you to consider.

Do you work well by yourself?

Working at home requires self-discipline and internal motivation. One of the biggest challenges of working at home is the isolation. There is no one to make you get to work on time, or keep you there. There are few people to raise your spirits when you are down, or to confer with when you need to make a decision. You'll need an independent spirit along with the ability to develop your own community of people to contact for support.

You'll want a good social network, because your job probably won't provide it for you. It helps a lot if you feel close to your immediate family, because in many ways they are your co-workers.

Do you have plenty of self-confidence?

Home-workers lack recognition in our society, so you'll need a certain amount of independence and self-confidence to continue believing in yourself. My husband and I work very hard running a mail-order business, which we used to do out of our home. The phone rang constantly, and it was a full-time job for both of us. In spite of this, my mother-in-law once asked my husband: "When are you going to go out and get a job?"

Often, other people don't respect the idea that you're "at work" when you're at home. Friends will come over and expect you to drop your work to spend time with them. A mother who works outside the home will ask you to watch her child for a while. Your partner may expect you to run errands and keep up the house during the day. You will have to define your work time and your work space for yourself and make your limitations clear to others.

You might want to develop a network of other people doing similar work and working at home. Jan and Charlie Fletcher of Next-Step Publications have several publications that give support to people working at home. One of their recent books is *Growing a Business, Raising a Family*, an anthology of articles on parenting and home businesses, drawn from their publications *New Families* magazine and *Home Business Advisor*.

Do you have a skill, interest, or trade that lends itself to working at home?

You can set up your own business or be employed by someone else. Either one will take some work. Choices range from crafts, child care, and typing to computer work, mail-order businesses, and insurance rating. Whatever you choose, enthusiasm and faith will help you get over many hurdles. If you believe in what you are doing, other things you need to do for your business will become clear to you.

Several good books are available. *The Work-At-Home Sourcebook*, by Lynie Arden, helps you find at-home work with companies all over the United States. *One Hundred and One Best Businesses*, by Sharon Kahn, gives ideas about starting your own business. *The Women's Work at Home Handbook: Income and Independence with a Computer*, by Patricia McConnel, specializes in using a computer to develop a home business. *Mail Order Moonlighting*, by Cecil C. Hoge Sr., gives information on mail-order businesses.

How will your work affect your family?

The support of your immediate family can make or break your project. Most home businesses don't neatly tuck away at 3 or 5 P.M. The telephone rings during dinner, and you occasionally need to finish up a project at night because your baby had a bad day. Home businesses also tend to spread themselves throughout the house.

If you have children, working any job is a challenge. Working at home is no different and is sometimes even harder. Your family will enjoy the ups you get when you feel creative or accomplished. They also will be there on your down days and when you feel overwhelmed. Will they support you then?

How are duties divided at your house?

Problems for people working at home can come from the unspoken agreements they have with their partners about housekeeping and child care. When one partner is home all day, he or she might be expected to watch the children and maintain the house, along with doing paid work. There is no way that anyone can maintain that kind of schedule for very long, and many home businesses fail or are abandoned because these problems aren't resolved.

If you are a woman considering home-based work, make agreements before beginning your new schedule. It will take some discipline to follow through on your plan. A messy house is a great excuse to put off a phone call you really should make. If people drop by my house, I just tell them I work during the day and clean house evenings and weekends like other employed moms. By cleaning together in the evenings, neither my husband or I feel overwhelmed by the task.

Can you work with your children around?

A few years ago I was looking for people to sew nursing clothing for *Motherwear*. Several mothers were interested in working for us, and thought working at home would be ideal. But within a short time, each one found that it was hard to work with their children around and that they really had much less "spare" time than they thought.

Most parents who work at home make arrangements so that they have some blocks of time without interruption. Children may be in school, or off with the other parent, or work can be done when the children are asleep. A good test if you are considering a home business with children around is to set yourself a good-sized project (maybe even planning your home business or preparing your résumé and work on it over several days. Record the time you work. Watch how often you are interrupted and how you deal with it. This should give you an idea of how much time you can work in a day and what other uses of your time you will be giving up in order to do it.

How will working at home affect your children?

If you have a baby or young children, working at home may seem like the ideal answer to your working dilemma. It seems as if you will be with them 24 hours a day and still earn money. But, reality may be very different. Instead of "being there for them" you may find your mind is constantly preoccupied with work, but it is a struggle to get any of it done!

It is easy to lose perspective and begin to see your children as an interference that keeps you from your work. Doing work with young children around requires the ability to plan carefully, prioritize your tasks, and return immediately to them after each interruption. As the children get older, you will have to clearly define your work times and areas and consciously make yourself available to your children at non-work times.

Getting your children involved in your work can be exciting for them. My six- and eight-year-olds earn all their pocket money stamping and labeling catalogs and doing other simple tasks for our business. They are learning responsibility and skills, and they enjoy buying what they want.

As far as children are concerned, there are advantages and disadvantages to working at home. A lot of it is in your attitude: if you are determined to be there for them, if you thrive on their day-by-day development, and if you find creative solutions to the home-versus-work conflicts that arise, working at home can be great for the whole family.

What are your zoning laws?

The zoning laws in your area and the home-work laws in your state are important points to consider before making your decision to work at home. Barbara Brabec, in her excellent book *Homemade Money*, outlines some of the laws and regulations you will have to deal with. It is a great book to read prior to start-up.

Do you have the time and money to invest in getting the business going?

Some businesses develop easily out of your prior work, but most home-based businesses require time and money to get them going. It isn't uncommon for a business to take several years to build to the point of supporting you. Some businesses take a substantial investment; others are cheap to start and you can expect to turn a profit quite quickly. If you don't have much money to invest, take your time starting your business and support yourself in other ways as it grows.

What's next?

If you still think working at home is for you, do a lot of reading and thinking before you start. Good planning and lots of knowledge steer you in the right direction, but your enthusiasm and your faith are the fuel that will get you there. ♥

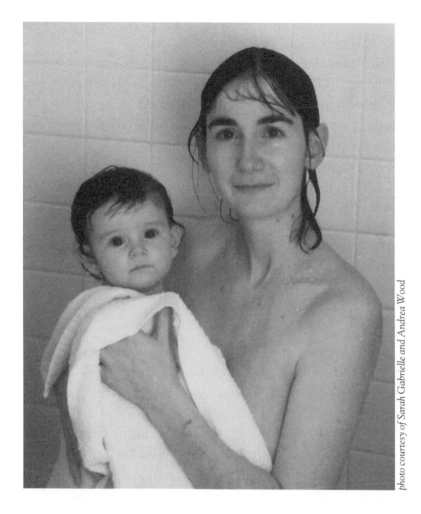

photo courtesy of Sarah Gabrielle and Andrea Wood

Mothers Share: Our readers discuss
Saving Money
COMPILED BY JODY WRIGHT

Raising children can be an expensive proposition. What's one way our readers save money at home? "Breastfeeding, of course!" People also found they could save money by using cloth diapers, whether they chose to wash them at home or use a diaper service.

Another popular way to save was by buying clothes from thrift stores, consignment stores, and on sale, and by using borrowed maternity clothes and hand-me downs. Many families save money by cooking food from scratch, growing their own produce, and eating less meat. Several families have started play groups to save money on child care.

Mothers Share asked: What ways have you discovered to save money at home?

"Collect coupons (only for items you can really use.) File them by product type in a coupon wallet with index tabs, and take them along whenever you shop. Combine them with store sales and double-coupon offers if possible. Don't discard any magazine until you've clipped all useful coupons."

"I stay at home, which has its benefits and its disadvantages: happy children and no child care expenses, but no income, either. I breastfeed, which I began only to save money (I got no support from family and friends). Now I am absolutely in love with breastfeeding—and my ten-month-old daughter."

"Staying with my kids saves money on daycare, transportation, wardrobe, taxes, and convenience items, and it saves my children from illnesses they would pick up in daycare."

"Diaper service is much less expensive than disposables, and it saves me valuable time."

"I recycle soft flannel receiving blankets by turning them into cloth diapers. I buy the blankets at yard sales and stitch them up like the pre-folded diapers. I also take nice, thick baby blankets that are pilled or faded from being washed and cover them with dollar-a-yard cotton to make quilt blankets."

"I made an inexpensive and convenient clothes hamper. I bought two pillowcases ($2.99) that matched the nursery and a pack of clothespin-type clips (69 ¢). We hook one case onto the end of the changing table, and when it's full, we replace it with the other one. We wash them with the clothes inside."

"Regular fitted crib sheets are often expensive, they never seem to fit once they're washed, and they can be chilly for a baby. I've started using flat flannel twin sheets instead. They're warmer, they can be purchased for half the price of crib sheets, and when your child moves to a regular bed, they are still useful. All I do for a crib mattress is fold the sheet in half and tuck the excess under."

"No packaged baby wipes—water is better!"

"I buy more expensive baby wipes that are hypoallergenic and use natural ingredients. Then I cut them in half and use them only when necessary."

"Take advantage of inexpensive or free entertainment: parks, bus or trolley rides, carousels, city walks. Go to the library rather than buying a lot of books. Find out when "free times" are at museums (most have them)."

"Create toys from cardboard boxes and water jugs."

"Use safe household objects as toys for your baby to explore."

"Try low-tech toys, home-made play dough, etc."

"Take a bath with your baby."

"Turn off the hot water heater until it's needed—our electric bill dropped by half!"

"Cook with less meat. We eat a lot of soup in the winter and a lot of salads and sandwiches in the summer, and we can our own fruit, jelly, pickles, etc."

"We put our weekly menu on the back of our grocery list. Then if we change the list because of a sale or special, we can change the menu. It used to be that we just bought more food and wound up wasting leftovers or things that didn't mix."

"Order bulk food through a natural foods distributor."

"Take your baby along whenever you can to save sitter costs."

"I added lace to my son's overalls for my daughter. Ruffles over the shoulder straps look darling. Little patches on the pockets—all this costs just a few dollars."

"I once worked for a podiatrist who told me that children should go barefoot until they are two years old."

"Have a swap-and-lend party where everyone brings items they don't currently use. A friend started a club where we meet once a month and swap coupons, baby clothes, books, toys and ideas with one another. We all have small children and this works great!"

"Cancel cable service and sell your TV. You've got more important things to do now."

"Use herbs and homeopathy, and don't depend on an M.D."

"Sleep with your baby and save on a crib, sheets, etc."

"Hang your laundry outside on nice days. Your energy costs go down, your diapers will get sterilized by the sun, and you'll get some fresh air and vitamin D!" ♥

Baby Camping

BY DIANE GREENING

When I was seven months old, my parents took me camping in the Great Smoky Mountains, not too far from home. They set up my playpen in a wing of their big green canvas tent. My father carried me in an army rucksack with two holes cut in the bottom for my feet, and my mother bathed me in the dishpan. She used to say, "I can never remember whether I washed you or the dishes first—or did it matter?"

In keeping with this family tradition, my husband and I took our son, Gawain, to the Catskills when he was ten weeks old. Although many people thought it was unusual for one so small to go camping, we found it surprisingly easy and enjoyable. I didn't have my mother's dishes-or-baby dilemma. I decided that for one weekend Gawain could survive with wet-washcloth baths.

Our modern dome tent, designed to be light in a backpack and simple to set up, could not hold a playpen and two adults, but it readily accommodated Gawain's cradle mattress and the stroller bag we used as his sleeping bag. The lucky boy was the only one who got to sleep in his own bed! An extra blanket and a hat kept him snug in the crisp fall weather.

Of course breastfeeding simplified things, both in camp and on the trail. I found the night feedings easier than they had ever been. When Gawain awoke, I only had to slip him out of his bag and into mine. The full moon shining through the tent provided adequate light; the wind in the trees and the murmuring brook gave us a special musical accompaniment.

Gawain's delight in camping showed in the morning, when he woke with a big smile at the sight of Mom sleeping right next to him. His eyes got even bigger as he took in the sight of the light-filled dome of the tent. This wasn't home, but it wasn't bad, either.

We traveled with friends and shared cooking and camp chores. The group ensured that there was always a spare pair of arms to cuddle a fussy baby. Gawain rode in luxury in front of Dad, getting a fine view of the Catskills. When he tired of the

photo courtesy of Diana Norman

journey, he simply fell asleep. I envied him his position toward the end of the day. My husband also carried some of the group's lunch load. The food on his back, he said, provided a necessary counterbalance to the baby on the front.

As I was just ten weeks postpartum, I carried only diapers and a generous supply of water for myself. (This had its down side: my pack was the only one that got heavier as the day wore on and the clean diapers were replaced by wet and dirty ones.) The diaper changing pad doubled as Gawain's "seat" when we stopped. During our lunch on Mt. Cornell, he lay happily on his back and kicked in the dappled forest light as we surveyed the brilliant fall colors. On the more exposed summit of Mt. Wittenberg, my backpack provided a screen from the sun and wind.

The advantages of camping in October were many. School had started and the temperatures hadn't yet gotten cold, so the crowds were gone and the weather was great for hiking. Bugs were non-existent, and trees were turning bright red and gold.

Everyone we met remarked on what a good camper Gawain was. It should not have come as a surprise. He was outside in the fresh air with many new sights, sounds, and smells to explore. He spent the days cradled close to Dad and the nights sleeping next to Mom. What more could a baby ask? ♥

The Best Toy Ever

BY ZIPORAH HILDEBRANDT

What is the ideal toy? It would hold your child's interest for a long time, much longer than two weeks. It would be age-appropriate to catch immediate interest and enhance developmental abilities. It would require a minimum of adult assistance or supervision, yet be versatile enough that when you do want to join in the fun, you can. It would be sturdy so your child outgrows it before it falls apart. And it would be inexpensive.

Here it is. It doesn't have a name. It's perfect for a range of age and development, from the slightly mobile squirmer to the running, leaping toddler. It graced our living room for over two years. It was crawled on, slid down, squirmed up, jumped off, jumped on, jumped over, pushed around, and run around. It was used as an obstacle course for children and pull toys, a foundation for caves and pillow piles, a table for snacks, and a lounger for reading stories.

You can't buy it in stores. But it can be made in less than an hour out of sturdy boxes and duct tape. And voila! Hours and hours of good times. ♥

How to Make the Best Toy Ever

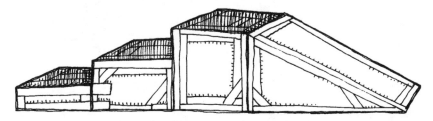

Choose sturdy boxes of the same width. (Don't use boxes with staples.) Cut them so you have three steps up. Use the bottoms of the boxes, as these are the sturdiest. Tape the steps together tightly inside and out. Use lots of duct tape to secure the high end of the slide to the top step. It's very important that the top step and slide be the same height at the top.

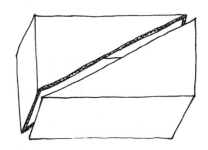

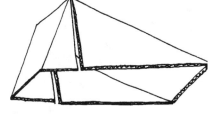

For the slide: cut a box on the diagonal, which seems to leave you with the wrong angle.

Now, make a vertical cut in the sides of the slide, bisecting the corner angle.

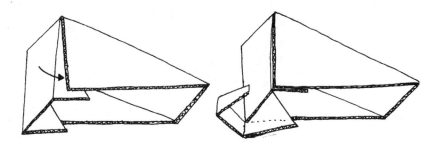

Slide the resulting flap behind the long side of the slide and trim off any excess from the bottom. The idea is that the high back end of the slide be perpendicular to the floor.

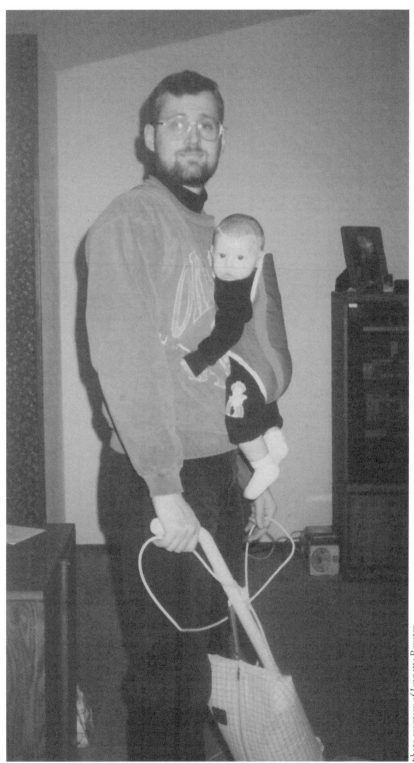

photo courtesy of Jennette Royster

Carriers

BY DAYNA J. HAMP

I t doesn't take a new mother long to discover she does not have enough arms to accomplish everything that is required of her. When little Jessica or baby Joey begins demanding attention, everything else just has to wait. Since none of us sprout extra limbs when a baby arrives, we must find other ways to make being a mom easier. A big help to me has been the baby carrier that holds my baby close while freeing my hands for other tasks.

There are three main features you should consider when shopping for a baby carrier.

1. Comfort. Look for one that puts most of the weight on your hips, easing the strain on your shoulders and back. Wide, well-padded shoulder straps will also alleviate shoulder discomfort.

2. Convenience. Try the carrier on to be certain it's easy to get your baby into it, get yourself into it, and take it off without assistance—and without losing your grip on your baby! Remember that attaching your carrier will become easier each time you use it.

3. Fit. The carrier should give plenty of support to an infant's back and head and fit snugly enough so your baby feels secure, yet allow plenty of breathing space. Openings should not be too tight around a baby's arms and legs.

Parents use carriers for taking walks, shopping, doing dishes, fixing supper, and innumerable other tasks. Babies love being carried, and will often rest their heads on Mama's or Papa's shoulder and go to sleep. I've found that each brand of carrier is different, so try them out and see what works for you. With practice, even those with seemingly complicated straps should prove useful, but if not—try another! With so many carriers on the market today, it pays to be a careful shopper. ♥

photo courtesy of Jan Kidd

The Home Learning Alternative

BY JODY WRIGHT

In the 1960s, John Holt's exploration of how children learn and why they fail in school challenged the world of education. After confronting problems in public and private education, Holt began working with alternative schools, but eventually became discouraged with these as well. He found even alternative schools perpetuating the stifling of children's curiosity, the regimentation of the group (required simply to keep order), the establishment of an adult-decided curriculum, and the loss of one-to-one interaction. Finally, he turned to home schooling and found it to be the answer to his lifelong quest.

Many parents who experience or anticipate frustration with public and private schools consider home schooling but soon dismiss it, believing it would require too much energy. If home-schooling parents had to plan a curriculum, correct papers, abide by a schedule, and meet long lists of criteria five days a week, it would be a huge task. But many of the activities that are typical of a school are based on the need to control a large group of students, keep fast and slow learners busy, contain everything in a classroom, plan a schedule well in advance, and begin and end within a specified period of time. Home schools are free of these limitations, so you can spend an afternoon at a science museum or in the woods, or put out an art project and do what needs to be done around the house.

Children have an innate curiosity and a fundamental desire to emulate those around them. These traits help them learn things at an incredible speed and can be well utilized in home schooling. My chief job as a home-schooling parent is to provide a stimulating environment for my children so they can follow their own curiosity and learn about the world. Parents provide examples through their work, their interests, and their own learning. Just going through an ordinary day in the presence of an active adult can be tremendously enriching.

There is a lot of time required, and for most families this will mean that one of you (if you are a two-adult family) can't work, which is hard in today's economy. As a home-schooling parent, you need to be available to your kids for much of their day. You need to be able to go places with them (museums, libraries, dance concerts, the theater) and to introduce them to the world around them. Most of the rest they will do themselves, just because they want to know. A lot of work? No, mostly a lot of fun and plenty of family time.

The reasons for home schooling are many. Home educators want their kids to learn different things than are taught in school or they want them to learn in a different way. Some people keep their children out of the early grades because they feel that five- to eight-year-olds should be playing and exploring, spending time outdoors and with those they love rather than sitting in a classroom doing paperwork. Others want to see children develop and utilize their individual curiosity instead of doing everything as a member of a group. Some feel they can raise their children in a more disciplined or religious environment, and others want to delay the introduction of their children to the "pseudo-culture" that exerts a strong influence at school. Some remove their children from the public or private schools as a way of addressing a child's special needs. Some families home school because they live too far from good schools.

Dorothy and Raymond Moore, authors of *Better Late than Early* and many other books on education, encourage parents to delay sending their children to school. Their experience has been that children who begin school in third grade are behind other children at the beginning of the year, but ahead of others by the end of the year. David and Micki Colfax, authors of *Homeschooling for Excellence*, have educated their children at home for fifteen years. Their first son graduated with high honors from Harvard and was the recipient of a Fulbright fellowship, and two others are currently attending Harvard. When home schoolers enroll in schools they often delight their teachers with their sincere interest in subjects and their self-discipline, since they have been in charge of their own time for so long.

One of the perceived challenges of home schooling is the lack of social interaction. But children who are not restricted to a school building all day are free to meet people of all ages. Apprenticing is common for older home schoolers, and classes or private sessions in many subjects are easy to schedule. Home schoolers can learn on the job or spend hours with a librarian or biologist researching a subject. Interacting in small groups with real intensity creates more meaningful friendships. As a result, home schoolers tend to be less motivated to please a group.

Of course there are challenges. Dealing with the authorities is one. Each state has different laws regarding home schooling. Some simply ask you to announce your intentions, while others require you to have your children tested, turn in curricula, keep records and portfolios, etc. In a few states you have to home school secretly. Authorities often feel threatened by what you are doing or don't understand your reasons for doing it. For most families, dealing with the system is an inescapable part of the process.

For a home schooling situation to be enjoyable, family dynamics need to be good. Periods of sibling fighting, isolation, or feeling overwhelmed alternate with enjoying strong family bonds, the fulfillment of social needs, and times of balance.

Circumstances are constantly changing as children grow and schedules change. These are the challenges of home schooling, but also they are the fodder for growth and education for the whole family. If we can build a strong base of good social interactions in the family, our children will take them out into the world with them.

One of the biggest challenges for me is trusting my inner beliefs in my children and waiting patiently for them to bloom. I need to talk to others with similar beliefs about children and home schooling. Sometimes I just need someone else to affirm for me how well my children are doing, to not feel so alone in this endeavor, to say, as many have, "You know, you must be doing something right, because they are some of the neatest kids I've ever met." ♥

TV: We're Working It Out

BY ZIPORAH HILDEBRANDT

A pre-school friend of my daughter's came to visit us once. Her first question was not "Where's your bathroom?" or "What's your cat's name?" but "Where's your TV?"

It's upstairs. We watch our favorite show for an hour each week. If my daughter's ill, she can watch *Sesame Street* or *Reading Rainbow*. We allow her four videos each week, to watch as she chooses.

Years of tantrums and of struggles with our differing values have led to this compromise. It works very well. My daughter doesn't expect a TV in every living room. But it's hard for me to reconcile my ideals with the world's reality. Televisions, VCRs, and the culture and values they represent are things I wish I didn't have to deal with. But, like sexism, racism, and politics, they won't go away by not participating.

When my daughter was born, we had no TV, and I was happy that way. My midwife was the first to recommend getting one, for those three- to five-hour-long nursings. I kept pillows, books, and water beside each arm of my rocking chair, instead.

Then we moved to a town with cable. I don't remember who suggested it first, but at that point, getting a television was okay with me. I was bored (I had no friends nearby and none at all with small children) and worn out by ill health and the constant company of a frenetic one-year-old. Every evening for three hours, my husband and I sat on the living room floor with our legs stretched out for our daughter to jump over, and watched public programming.

Then I turned on *Oprah* in the afternoons for a little contact with the adult world, then *Sesame Street* to see what the big deal was. My little one ran up to the screen every five minutes, laughed, and ran away again. How could that damage her? And I liked it. It was the funniest thing in my day at the time.

There were other entertaining shows: French for kids, Mister Rogers. It was fun. It was easy. My daughter began to get strange ideas about gender roles: Only female monsters wear clothes; only boys have short hair. Every shopping trip included a tense scene when we said good-bye to whatever *Sesame Street* figure we'd encountered.

Later, there were commercials, viewed at the neighbor's house. Result: "I want this. I have to have this."

"Where on earth did you see this?" Garish box. Incomprehensible purpose. Dubious value.

"On TV." By the time my daughter was three, I'd had it. I canceled the cable. Tears. Screams. "Heartless," people said. No more Bert and Ernie? Begging. Whining. Everyone else still had a TV—daycare, neighbors, friends, the other kids at the playground and grocery store. "Tough," I said. I didn't miss it.

Then my husband came home with a VCR. (Surprise.) We set limits. We didn't stick to them. We set new limits. We lost track of what limit we'd set last. My husband and I had different standards of what was okay, different tolerances for pleading. I faced reality. I like an occasional movie as much as anyone. I don't like arguments with my husband.

If I could do it all over again, I would never have turned on the TV to begin with. But, to be honest, I have to ask myself, "Whose problem is this?" Yes, I have concerns about health, time spent passively, potential vision problems, attention span, violence, gender roles, and cultural values I don't approve of. But my daughter is a happy, active, imaginative child. She experiences violence first-hand on the school playground and responds appropriately. The gender stereotypes in most picture books are just as bad as anything in Disney. And there's nothing wrong with her attention span.

My unhappiness with our compromises is my problem. I could assert myself, make my values the family's values. I don't keep my objections to myself; neither do I insist on my way being the only right way. I share my concerns when our daughter wants more TV time. We negotiate. I have deeper values about love and caring, about children knowing what's good for them and communicating that knowledge to their parents in ways we cannot fully and consciously understand. I value trust over rigidity. Circumstances can take precedence over structure.

My commitment to parenting is not a commitment to a set of rules or ideas, it's a commitment to a person who changes and grows every day in unfathomable, miraculous ways. Every family is unique. Every child has her own needs, propensity, and talents. Every parent has individual values and a unique perspective on life. I value honoring those differences between us and finding common ground. For me, being a parent has often meant letting go of "my way" in order to listen. Maybe someday we'll put the TV away for a while. I hope so. But meanwhile, I'll let go and listen. ♥

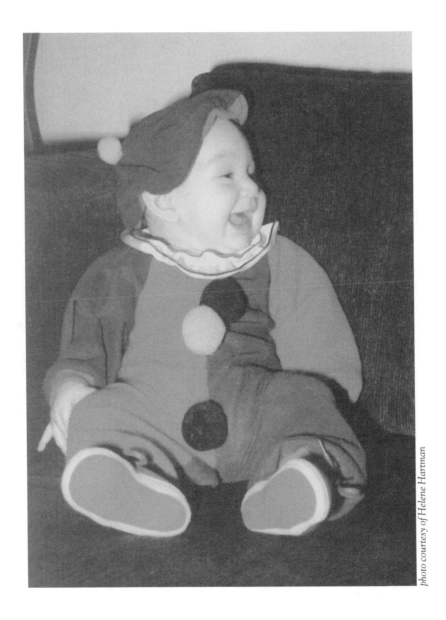

photo courtesy of Helene Hartman

photo courtesy of Gabrielle Shatan

You

Whether or not you knew it at the time, your decision to have children meant giving up a great deal of your personal time and space. It's practically an inevitable byproduct of motherhood: you lose your self, at least temporarily. Some of us let go easily; others are always looking to get a little back.

Somewhere behind round-the-clock nursings, keeping up with the home, orchestrating the family schedule, and responding to everyone else's needs, the lone you still lurks. It won't be long before your children's demands begin to diminish. It's important for this reason—and also for your sanity—that you find time to be alone, to take care of yourself, and to maintain your individuality. In addition to feeling responsible for everybody else, you are responsible for you, and you alone must attend to that.

The Baby and the Appointment Book

BY THERESA RODRIGUEZ FARRISI

After the undertaking of pregnancy and the work of birthing, the challenge most mothers face is the overhaul of routine and schedule, the loss of solitude and the mourning of it: the overwhelming state that early motherhood brings. This most rewarding and demanding of life's vocations requires on-the-job training, virtually all-day (and often all-night) hours, seven days a week, unendingly. It requires new plans and focus—from the outward world of job or career or school to the inward world of home and family. Time becomes a rare commodity to parcel or invest painstakingly.

In those days of new motherhood, the responsibilities and tasks required of a diminished supply of energy can really tax the sensibilities! It seems we have twice as much to do and half the time to do it. I offer the following philosophy, which I call "Reformed Relaxitude," in hopes that the joys and rewards of motherhood will exceed abundantly above the toils and drudgeries.

Do less in a day than you used to.

This may mean simply getting you and baby clean, fed, and dressed or making only one business call, not ten. It might mean reading just one chapter of a book, rather than relaxing for hours in the evening. Rarely are there large blocks of time anymore, so accept serendipitous moments as the chance for a *little* reading, a *little* artistic endeavor, or a *little* sleep. Let go of that urge to GET IT ALL DONE...NOW. Never let what you have to do (or didn't get to do) cause you to resent the baby you love. It isn't worth it, and it doesn't matter right now.

Keep a little notebook with you and write down everything you think about doing, calls you want to make, things to buy. This will eliminate the frustration of having half the brain you used to, if you're like me.

Accept motherhood for what it is.

You won't get good grades or a paycheck for an orderly home, a decent dinner, sorted laundry, or surviving a long night of teething or colic. These are, perhaps, the quiet

photo courtesy of Jennette Royster

glories of past ages. Mothers from the beginning have done all you are doing now: changing and washing diapers, cooking, walking around with the baby, rocking, waking at night, knowing baby's soft skin, seeing those little eyes roll back when she nurses, experiencing the loveliness of being loved and being received so fully and simply. Do not overlook such banalities of life, for in the very living and doing of what is common to all you will find your compensation and reward.

Restructure your household chores.

Each of my three children needed a carrier until the age of four or five months. I've held them while washing dishes (with one hand), sweeping, doing laundry. Later, when their heads were upright, I used a backpack to keep both hands free. Babies just want to be near their mothers, after all, and be with them whatever they are doing.

Have you noticed that if the dishes are done the rest of the house doesn't look so bad? Try attacking this series of tasks in the following order: toilet (daily), dishes, clothes off floors and furniture, other things off floors and furniture. With made beds the place looks pretty good. This keeps everything a step above chaos. Remember the rule "Don't put it down, put it away."

Can you get a cordless phone and/or answering machine? I'm not an avid lover of screened phone calls, but sometimes you've just got to forget you have a phone. That also means staying off of it. But if you're on it, a cordless phone is wonderful. You can talk while you're nursing, doing dishes, fixing food, sitting in the yard, changing a diaper. . . .

Don't forget your body.
It helps to consume calming foods and drinks. If you have trouble sleeping, a liberal amount of honey before bed is a good soporific. Try to get a hot soak before bed. Order out, or buy healthy convenience foods, if you need to. Meals made with simple ingredients can be made interesting with spices and flavorings. No one has to make everything from scratch; you needn't feel guilty about this!

Get outside every day.
. . . but consolidate your efforts so you don't need to make multiple trips. You realistically need one-half hour to get each person ready, so leave plenty of time when preparing for an outing.

Change expectations; know your limitations.
Learn to say "No," "I'm sorry," and "I can't." It is here that it is prudent to find the balance between the urgent, the necessary, and the desirable. You cannot be what you once were; that is gone. What remains and thrives is the fruition of your years of growth, the fullness and maturity.

It is healthy sometimes just to stay in bed, ignore the clock, and love your baby. Perhaps this is why our family has evolved into late risers; we all love to lie around in our (family) bed snuggling and cuddling and enjoying one another. I am by no means making a universal call to laziness, just a call to recognize and pursue what really matters. These are precious moments that are all too fleeting. I make no apologies for the time I have spent nurturing, stimulating, holding, teaching, touching, playing (and praying) with my little ones.

Perhaps I am suggesting a new attitude about your identitiy and course of life. Receive motherhood as a joy and a priviledge, not as a burden; cultivate thankfulness for things both large and small; remember someone with more hardship or inconvenience than you have, and keep it all in perspective. Look for opportunities to do something for someone else: it keeps you from feeling sorry for yourself. Remember how much you longed to have this baby. And in your longing fulfilled, you will be enriched by the changes, graced by the challenges, and deepened by the riches of being a mother. ♥

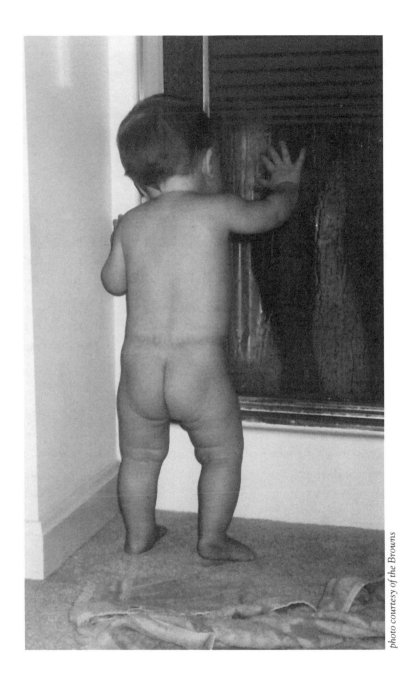

Take a Break

BY JODY WRIGHT

"I need a break!" It's a common plea of people with young children . . . and certainly an understandable one. Babies have needs around the clock; as parents we have to make sure we get the breaks we need to maintain our sanity.

Plan something for yourself each day.

What is really important to you? A warm bath? Time to read? A walk? A phone call or visit with a friend? Perhaps you can work one or more of these into your schedule without involving anyone else. It is very important, with a new little one needing so much of your time, to find time for the things that relax you and give you pleasure.

Get help from your partner and extended family.

Never underestimate this one! Letting partners, families, and close friends develop relationships with your baby will provide you with breaks for years to come. Start with short periods, perhaps ten or twenty minutes at first. Before long a half-hour walk will be quite acceptable, and when the baby is toddling, several hours should be no problem.

When you leave, make sure your child's needs are met.

The secret to successful breaks is making sure your child's emotional needs are met. Before making plans, consider what type of arrangement would be acceptable to your child and what wouldn't. If you push your child away from you too fast or for too long, your breaks will be followed by increased clinginess and frustration, and your own needs won't be filled at all.

Have a caretaker be with your child in your own home or another familiar environment. Consider having someone care for your child in your home while you are there. For my children and me, this took away the anxiety of separation, while still giving me a chance to get some work done. When they needed me, I was close at hand. This is also a good way for you to get to know a sitter, so you can guide her or him in caring for your child the way that is important to you.

When you are going out, look for a time of day that is good for your child. A

photo courtesy of Adrienne Keranen

matinee movie or an early dinner that brings you back before bedtime can be much easier for children than an outing that requires them to go to sleep without you.

Always explain what is going on, and say good-bye to your child. Even an infant will understand what you are trying to communicate. Though sneaking out may seem easier in the short run, your long-term goal is to have children who trust you. By saying good-bye every time, you will let them know that they don't have to worry constantly that you may be sneaking off. (And whatever tears ensue almost always dry up soon after you're gone!)

Don't feel afraid to change your mind and not go out if your child is too upset. I have found that responding to my children's fears about separation has increased their willingness to let me go in the future. They can say, "It's all right for you to go out tonight, Mom," if they trust that I will respond when it isn't.

Find new ways to take vacations.

Sometimes you just need a break from routines. If you don't feel that your little ones are ready to be separated from you for an extended period, there are many wonderful places to vacation together. Breastfed babies travel easily, because there's no need to worry about food preparation. And if your children are used to sleeping with you, even a new bed feels secure if you're all in it!

Does traveling with a baby sound overwhelming? Take a vacation at home! Choose a weekend and plan some sightseeing and entertainment nearby. Unplug the phone, ignore the dishes, call out for pizza, go out for breakfast, and enjoy relaxing and playing with one another. You can use familiar sitters if you need some time alone during your weekend "away."

How about a twelve-hour vacation? This has been a lifesaver for me. I make arrangements with my husband and others to care for the children. Then I plan a day doing just the kinds of things I crave: a massage, a quiet lunch with a friend, time to write in my journal, a walk, a counseling appointment, perhaps some shopping. I plan activities to rejuvenate myself. If I need to go home and nurse my baby during the day, I do. Otherwise I nurture myself from 9 A.M. to 9 P.M. and get back in time to put the kids to bed.

Parenting is a twenty-four-hour-a-day job. But when you need a break, it's only fair to you (and your family, in the long run) to take one! ♥

Motherwear photo

Exercising During Pregnancy—and After

BY ALICIA MᶜDONALD

Pregnancy and postpartum offer a special opportunity for a woman to focus on her body. The physical transformations that come from nurturing a new life can be regarded as miraculous and beautiful, overwhelming and frustrating, a loss of the pre-pregnant shape, or all of the above! Exercise offers both physical and psychological benefits that can help women integrate the radical changes of childbearing. Regular exercise can increase confidence and bring comfort to body and mind. Here are some basic rules for exercise in the maternal year.

Think about what kind of exercise is enjoyable and comfortable. You might like the 90 percent weightlessness of swimming, and it's virtually injury-free. Or you may prefer walking, dancing, or exercise classes. A class setting can provide the discipline to make exercise a regular part of your life, and the friendships gained in a group of your peers are a wonderful benefit, especially for first-time mothers. Whatever you choose, you will find that the subtle aches, pains, and fatigue of pregnancy and postpartum often disappear after a workout.

Make sure your medical care provider agrees that exercise will benefit you and the baby (or babies!). Start any new exercise program gradually, and don't make any drastic changes in intensity (like taking up jogging). Here are some specifics to keep in mind.

• Be careful about stretching and certain yoga postures, as your hormones have made you more vulnerable to muscle strain. Warm up at the start of a routine, then stretch a little. Any good aerobic routine (including swimming) should start and end gradually.

• Stay focused on your breathing, inhaling more deeply as your body moves faster. If you feel any pain or a lot of Braxton-Hicks contractions, walk around and then stop. Your breathing should be back to normal before you stop or sit down.

• Gauge your workout by assessing your working heart rate. Take 10-second pulse counts at your wrist or neck. As a general rule, pregnant women should manage their exercise routine so that the count stays under 24 (144 beats per minute). In water, it should stay below 21 (126 beats per minute), and postpartum it should stay below 27 (162 beats per minute). The aerobic portion of a workout should not last more than 25 minutes in pregnancy and 40 minutes postpartum.

• Stretch at the end of the workout, then lie on your left side for a few minutes to relax.

• After 26 weeks of pregnancy, don't exercise flat on your back for more than five minutes at a time. If you are short of breath or uncomfortable, move to a sitting or side-lying position for abdominals. Concentrate on pelvic tilts either standing or on hands and knees. Hold your abdominal muscles tightly as you exhale and tilt.

• Drink eight to ten glasses of water every day, and you'll feel better while exercising. Make sure you eat within two hours of an exercise session, because pregnant and lactating moms burn more glucose. In pregnancy, the idea is *not* to burn calories and lose weight!

• Get plenty of rest and try to keep stress down. Ask for help or time off when you need it.

• Do not work out in very hot weather or when you are running a fever, as the baby has no way to dissipate its body heat.

• Do not exercise if there is any leaking vaginal fluid or spotting.

• Wear special exercise clothing and play great music to boost your spirits. Make free use of props (pillows, chairs, couches, mats).

• After birthing your baby, wait until your red bleeding has stopped. (That could be two weeks to three months.) You will know when you feel ready. Remember that moving will help with fatigue and depression. Until that time, floor routines, such as abdominal curl-ups (crossing each elbow to the opposite knee), leg lifts, stretching, and "Kegels" are helpful.

• Wear a supportive bra and try to breastfeed before you exercise.

Have fun! You'll feel great when you're finished. ♥

Time Management for Moms

BY JODY WRIGHT

When I find myself falling behind in my responsibilities or feeling very disorganized, I often turn to time management books for inspiration. But not all of their ideas are realistic for the job of mothering. You can't "delegate more work to your secretary," or "leave your desk clean and your organized To-Do List where you'll see it as soon as you arrive in the morning." So, I've come up with some of my own ideas for how to survive and thrive with a business, children, and an unquenchable desire to do interesting things with my life.

Survival Strategies

• *Simplify.* The fact is, you can't do what you did before this little bundle arrived in your life. There is no way around that. There is so much pressure now for new mothers to return to jobs, for the house to be neat, and for obligations to be met. But the reality is that Junior keeps you awake every night and your energy is rapidly being depleted!

You don't have to do everything, but if you want sanity, you have to do the *important* things. Think through what the essential tasks are, and make deliberate decisions to do these and not the others. Come up with ways the essentials can be simplified or combined with other projects. No one is going to loose sleep because the clean clothes aren't folded. We simply sort ours into baskets, which is where they often stay until used.

• *Go Back Twenty-Seven Times.* Every time I have a new baby I am reminded of this basic time-management maxim. Infants, particularly, seem to have no patience for your activities and want you *immediately*! You soon learn that the likelihood of your getting any uninterrupted time is just about nil, so you might as well use what you've got! Pick a task that is top priority for you, get started, and keep returning to it until it is done, even if it takes twenty-seven times!

• *Fill the Real Need.* When a child fusses or asks for something, try to tune in to what her *real* need is. Two children fighting? Perhaps what they *really* need is a change of scenery or a snack. Instead of just dealing with the "presenting problem," try uncovering the underlying need, and make sure it is filled. If you get it right, you've given yourself another twenty minutes! Many times children just want to be near you. Let them set up shop nearby for a little while, and everyone will be happy.

If you need to delay a minute in order to finish what you're doing, communicate your need to your child. "It sounds as if you're hungry. As soon as I finish typing this paragraph I'll help you get a snack." Conveying how much you care about his needs does wonders for helping him meet *your* needs.

An important thing to remember is that you often get only what time is left after everybody else's needs are met. If you don't figure out how to satisfy their physical and emotional needs, yours won't be satisfied either.

• *Fill Their Tanks*. Though feeding kids often is pretty important if you want any peace in your house, this is about their *emotional* tanks. Kids need a lot of hugs and kisses, listening ears, and pats on the back. I find that if my little ones have enough of these, I can practically take a day off! That is why I like to organize my day to start out slowly. As each child wakes up I try to take time to check in with her and offer some caresses. "Good morning, sunshine, how are you feeling today? Was that you in our bed in the middle of the night? Did you have a scary dream?" Accented with some warm hugs and kisses on the top of the head, a snuggle in bed, or a nursing, five to ten minutes per child seems to make their day. (Then again, maybe it makes *my* day!)

Got a fussy or bored child? Try taking him off by himself for some one-to-one time. This works better than any time-out!

• *Mirror Image*. My mother taught me this. I remember her telling me when I was disgruntled, "Just start acting the way you want to feel, and pretty soon you'll feel that way. Put a smile on your face and everyone will smile back." I didn't have the ability at that time to separate myself from my feelings, but now I know that if we are all feeling "feisty" (as we call it in our family), it is only temporary. I've found it is even more temporary if I decide to rise above my negative feelings.

• *Round Robin*. Sometimes when things have gotten really hectic, and we parents finally arrange some time just to be with the kids, it seems as if all hell breaks loose. Everybody seems to be weepy, angry, or fighting. Then I remind myself that this just shows how much we need to be together. I step into my Nice Counselor role and say, "O.K., everyone gets a chance to talk. Take two minutes to say what you're feeling." We go around the circle, starting with the most vocal or emotional child. We listen to anything she has to share, and move on when it feels right. The whole process usually gets everyone feeling heard and loved again.

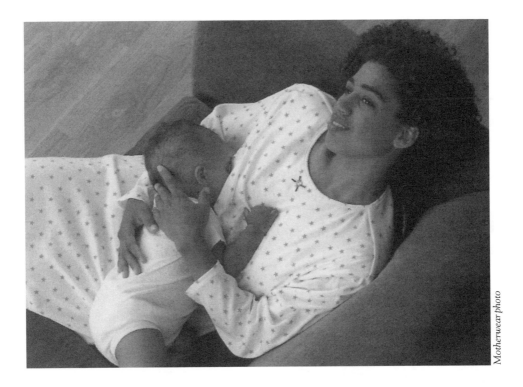

Motherwear photo

But now let's get past the social aspects of finding time for our work and into the more traditional time-management skills.

Getting the Big Picture

"I've just got to have some time to myself. I can't see the big picture!" Do you ever feel that way? You may have to have some time alone to formulate your goals.

• Start by writing down everything that is really important to you (raising a happy family, being successful in your career, going back to school, moving to another house, etc.). Remember, these are *goals*, not *tasks*.

• Look over what you've written and choose your three or four most important goals. Which ones are right for this time in your life? Be realistic.

• Under each goal, write down the tasks you would need to do in order to achieve those goals. Put this list in a prominent place, and include these tasks as part of your list of things to do every day.

Getting Things Done

• Make a list. There were probably many things you expected to get when you had kids: warmth, affection, intimacy, purpose, and much more. And you got those things. What you didn't count on was what you'd have to trade for them: time alone, control of your life, the ability to think clearly, your own space, etc. A to-do list is a step toward getting those back, gaining some control over your life. It helps to make some decisions before they are all made for you.

A notebook really helps me get organized. I love those fancy ones with places to stick a pen, an extra key, and a checkbook. But the fact is, a lot of the pre-printed pages are designed for executives with secretaries, not mothers with children. So a good, sturdy (so the baby can chew on it, and the toddler draw on it) notebook or spiral pad does just as well with much less expense.

Now, sit down, get comfortable, and start relieving your mind of all the things you are afraid you are going to forget to do. Once you have everything down, start organizing it. Put an "A" before each task that has to be done right away, a "B" before each item that you would like to get done sometime soon, and a "C" before everything that can wait.

A good rule of thumb is that accomplishing about 20 percent of the items on your to-do list should satisfy about 80 percent of your immediate needs. The other 80 percent of the items carry only about 20 percent of the weight as far as urgency goes. Since you have only about 20 percent of the time that you used to have, you either have to do only the most important things or do the most important part of several things.

• Go down your list and decide which things, realistically, you aren't going to do. Cross them out. Are there B's and A's that, no matter how important, you probably won't do anyway? Here's your chance to be honest with yourself!

• Consider which things you could get someone else to do. This requires making arrangements, but each task someone else does frees up your time for work that only you can do.

• Now look at all your A's. If you only had time to do a few of those, which would provide the most rewards? Mark these as A-1's, and do them first.

If you are still feeling overwhelmed, get out a new piece of paper and copy only the most important items from your to-do list: the things you really want to get done today or this week. Those are the only ones you have to face right now.

The Importance of You

In most households, the family revolves around Mom. If Mom is healthy, happy, and fulfilled, the rest of the family will be, too. Put aside that worn-out ethic that you have to give up everything for the family, that you get only the left-overs. Every day, in some way, you need to put your needs first. It isn't your family's responsibility to fill your needs, it is yours. And fulfilling your own needs sets a good example that helps everyone else fulfill theirs.

Getting control of your own time by simplifying, organizing, and prioritizing will, in the long run, be beneficial for you and for everyone around you. You'll probably never have a clean desk, a devoted secretary, and a prioritized to-do list waiting for you at 8 A.M., but you *can* have a simpler household, a clearer idea of your goals, kids who give you a few minutes to do work, and some priorities to guide you through your days—and your parenting years. ♥

photo courtesy of Catherine and Aaron Freund

Chapter One: Loving, Caring, and Bonding

Showing Love to Our Children, ©1989, Jody Wright. All rights reserved.
Marsupial Parenting, ©1990, Beth Hersh. All rights reserved.
Listening to Babies, ©1989, Vimala McClure. All rights reserved.
Forming a Loving Bond with Your Baby, ©1993, Jody Wright. All rights reserved.
Seeing Them Whole, ©1992, Beth Hersh. All rights reserved.
Why Your Baby Loves to Be Touched, ©1992, Jody Wright. All rights reserved.
Take a Bath With Your Baby, ©1993, Motherwear. All rights reserved.
Want to Massage Your Baby? Just Do It! ©1993, Just Do It! Jody Wright. All rights reserved.
Infant Massage: A Way to Show You Care, ©1989, Jody Wright. All rights reserved.
Babies Love Sounds, ©1993, Ziporah Hildebrandt. All rights reserved.
"And Then What Happened?" Telling Stories to Children, ©1993, Motherwear. All rights reserved.
The Most Perfect Baby in the Whole Wide World, ©1992, Jody Wright. All rights reserved.

Chapter Two: Breastfeeding

The Magic of Milk, ©1989, Beth Hersh. All rights reserved.
Why Is Breastfeeding So Important? ©1994, Jody Wright. All rights reserved.
The Message Is Love, ©1989, Beth Hersh. All rights reserved.
The Elements of Breastfeeding Success, ©1992, Jody Wright. All rights reserved.
Mothers Share: The Challenges of Nursing, ©1990, Jody Wright. All rights reserved.
Lay a Strong Foundation for Breastfeeding Success, ©1994, Ziporah Hildebrandt. All rights reserved.
The Amazing Health Benefits of Nursing, ©1994, Jody Wright. All rights reserved.
Nursing the Adopted Baby, ©1990, Jody Wright. All rights reserved.
Tandem Nursing, ©1994, Amy Mager. All rights reserved.
Mothers Share: Expressing Your Milk, ©1989, Jody Wright. All rights reserved.
How Breastfeeding Saves You Money, ©1990, Jody Wright. All rights reserved.
The Art of Discreet Nursing, ©1989, Jody Wright. All rights reserved.
Mothers Share: Nursing in Public, ©1991, Jody Wright. All rights reserved.
When It's Time to Wean, ©1990, Beth Hersh. All rights reserved.

Chapter Three: Parenting

Something Wonderful About Toddlers, ©1990, Beth Hersh. All rights reserved.
Helping Children Express Their Feelings, ©1990, Jody Wright. All rights reserved.
Becoming a Sibling, ©1990, Beth Hersh. All rights reserved.
Treating Children as Equals, ©1989, Jody Wright. All rights reserved.
A Fine Line: Popular Culture, Gender Roles and Our Children, ©1994, Ziporah Hildebrandt. All rights reserved.
Magic Moments, ©1993, Beth Hersh. All rights reserved.
The Tao of Motherhood, ©1991, Vimala McClure. All rights reserved.

Chapter Four: Survival

Getting Ready for the First Six Weeks, ©1989, Jody Wright. All rights reserved.
The Challenges of Parenting a Baby, ©1993, Jody Wright. All rights reserved.
Colic and Allergy: A Trying Time, ©1993, Motherwear. All rights reserved.
Dealing with Postpartum Blues, ©1991, Judy Snyder. All rights reserved.
Surviving Postpartum Depression, ©1991, Motherwear. All rights reserved.
How to Survive a Fussy Baby, ©1990, Beth Hersh. All rights reserved.
Don't Sweat It: Tips for Summer Sanity, ©1992, Andrea Collins. All rights reserved.
Taking It Out on the Kids, ©1991, Beth Hersh. All rights reserved.
Mothers Share: Handling Criticism, ©1990, Jody Wright. All rights reserved.
A Nursing Mom's Holiday Survival Guide, ©1993, Ziporah Hildebrandt. All rights reserved.
Our Little Lamb Is a Goat, ©1991, Carol Hubbard House. All rights reserved.

Chapter Five: Sleep

How Does Your Baby Sleep?, ©1989, Jody Wright. All rights reserved.
Uncovering the Myths About Shared Beds, ©1989, Beth Hersh. All rights reserved.

Motherwear:
A company that's much more than its catalog

Motherwear was developed to support breastfeeding mothers as women, nurturers, wives, homemakers, and professionals. By doing this, we support families. By supporting families we hope to make a difference in the world. Our goal is to offer parents knowledge and tools to enhance their family life through early bonding, breastfeeding, and loving parenting. We are committed to the encouragement and support of nurturing families in our local and global communities.

At Motherwear, we make breastfeeding fashionable with beautiful clothes for nursing mothers. Our free, full-color, mail order catalog offers top-quality garments designed with hidden nursing openings that allow easy access for discreet breastfeeding — anytime, anywhere. Our exclusive selection of styles, fabrics, and sizes are carefully chosen for durability, practicality, and beauty. In our catalog you will also find an extensive selection of nursing bras in sizes 32A to 46J as well as sleep bras. A wide range of breast pumps, support pillows, diapering supplies, and children's clothes makes Motherwear the complete catalog for the nursing mother.

In addition to the catalog, Motherwear publishes two free nursing guides, valuable tools for new moms. Our magazine, *Parenting from the Heart*, is also free. It provides information and inspiration for parents of young children and was the source of articles for this book.

From our free literature to our financial assistance with La Leche League's help line, from the hundreds of customers we assist every day to the dozens of employees we call "family," we're always trying to give our very best. As a member of Businesses for Social Responsibility, we are dedicated to fostering company policies that serve our communities, both local and global.

If you would like to receive a copy of our catalog, our nursing guides or *Parenting from the Heart* magazine please call 1-800-633-0303 or write Motherwear, 320 Riverside Drive, Northampton, MA 01060.